Prisoner of Zion

Muslims, Mormons, and Other Misadventures

Scott Carrier

 COUNTERPOINT
BERKELEY

Library of Congress Cataloging-in-Publication is available.
ISBN 978-1-61902-121-1

Cover design by Michael Kellner
Interior design by Neuwirth & Associates

COUNTERPOINT
1919 Fifth Street
Berkeley, CA 94710
www.counterpointpress.com

Printed in the United States of America
Distributed by Publishers Group West

10 9 8 7 6 5 4 3 2 1

That this social order with its pauperism, famines, prisons, gallows, armies, and wars is necessary to society; that still greater disaster would ensue if this organization were destroyed; all this is said only by those who profit by this organization, while those who suffer from it—and they are ten times as numerous—think and say quite the contrary.

—Leo Tolstoy

The Kingdom of God is within you.

—Jesus, Luke 17:21

Table of Contents

Prisoner of Zion

Before the snow falls
the smell of the furnace
burning the summer's dust.

Scene One

Sunday morning, 1962, a family restaurant.

A husband, wife, and two young sons are eating lunch after attending church. The mother is dressed like Jackie Kennedy—white pillbox hat, long white gloves. The father wears a black suit like Joe Friday on *Dragnet*. The boys have black suits like their father's, and crew cuts, freckles, and glasses that are taped together and hang sideways on their noses. The boys are uncomfortable in their Sunday clothes. The father is uncomfortable with his family.

The mother asks her sons, "Well, what did you learn from the sermon this morning?"

"The minister was saying God listens to our prayers," says the younger son, age five, "so I was praying, asking God to move the light hanging from the ceiling, as a sign. Nothing happened."

"I don't believe in God," says the older son, age six.

The mother is shocked. "Don't say that. There most certainly is a God."

"It's a lie," the boy says. "There is no God." He's angry.

The father is adding up the check, making sure the numbers are correct. The younger son looks out the window to the gas station across the street where a man is filling his tank.

The man bursts into flames.

The son looks at his dad. "They made a mistake," he says. "They overcharged us by $2.38."

The boy looks back to the man in flames, and he's rolling over and over on the asphalt, trying to put himself out.

Inside the Momosphere

Most cities are built on flat ground where buildings and trees block the view of the horizon, but Salt Lake City sits in a valley between two separate mountain ranges and has something of the shape of a bowl. Inside this bowl, no matter where you are, you can see every other place in the bowl—to distances of twenty miles—but nothing beyond it, unless you get up on the rim, on top of the mountains. From there you can see the curve of the Earth.

This is what I'm used to, living in a bowl, a high desert basin. When I leave town and spend time in flat places I start getting claustrophobic because everything is close up and nothing is far away, and if I stay too long I have panic attacks. I tell this to my friends who live in flat places and they say it is I who live in a claustrophobic place—among the Mormons. "How can you live there?" they say, meaning, How can you live surrounded by religious fanatics?

This makes me defend the Mormons, as they are much like people everywhere else—some are bad, some are good.

It doesn't bother me that Mormons believe God grew up as a human being on a planet circling a sun called Kolob. I'm not upset when they tell me He came to Earth in a physical body and had sex with the Virgin Mary. These beliefs, as Jefferson said, neither pick my pocket nor break my bones. And when it comes right down to it, some of the most liberal minds I know come from Mormon families—men and women who would be careful before criticizing what they don't understand.

I have a problem with only one of their beliefs—that Mormons are God's chosen people and He gave this land to them. This is Zionism, and I'm against it, wherever it occurs, because it's nothing but a lie used to justify taking land and liberty from other people. This does pick my pocket and break my bones, and I hope someday it'll be seen by everyone as a ridiculous and archaic notion, similar to the belief that the Earth is flat.

I'm working on a screenplay, one where God appears with a bag of golf clubs in the apartment of a successful New York public relations executive and says He wants to kill himself because He's always been a lousy god and He thinks everybody will be better off without Him. There are other planets, He says, run by other gods, and their people are happy. And this isn't the first time he's failed. He's had other planets in the past and they didn't turn out well either. He just kept thinking He could do better next time. He comes to the PR executive because He's realized He can't actually commit suicide, says He tried it and it didn't work, so He's decided the next best thing to do is ruin His image, make it so nobody wants to pray to Him ever again.

"All we got to do is tell them the truth," He says.

The PR executive asks God why He has golf clubs, and God says He thought they could get in some rounds while they're going over the details of the media campaign. God says He's been working on his game and that He plays as a human, not as an all-powerful being, for religious reasons. When they get out on the course it turns out God isn't very good at all. He misses shots and gets really angry and pounds His clubs into the grass yelling, "God damn it!"

The plan is to bring back Walter Cronkite and have him announce on the six o'clock news that God is a big failure and wants to quit, followed by an exclusive, commercial-free interview with the deity Himself. In the interview God says He now realizes it was wrong to keep starting new religions, telling different people they were His chosen ones and then giving them a bunch of land where other people were already living. In His confession He breaks down and says, "I just wanted my children to be happy. I just wanted them to love me."

I've tried to leave Salt Lake, many times, but I always come back. Now, after living here for nearly fifty years, I'm starting to think this landscape has become a part of my body and I need to see the mountains—Lone Peak, Twin Peaks, Mt. Olympus—in order to feel whole. I watch how they change shape with the light. On a clear morning after a snowstorm they rise up like a wave about to crash down on the city; in the summer haze they are so small and far away.

This isn't how it is for most people who live here. Among the Mormons it's not the mountains that are important but Temple Square, downtown. It's an entire city block, a perfect square, seven hundred and fifty feet long on a side, surrounded by a wall twelve feet high. Inside the wall is the neo-Gothic Salt Lake Temple, which is the center of the Mormon metaphysical cosmology. This is very important, and yet it takes people a long time to learn. For members of the LDS Church, the Salt Lake City Temple is the hub around which everything that means anything revolves. Their identity, their purpose, is embodied there inside the wall.

The Tabernacle is also in there, a beautiful egg-like building, home of the longest-running radio show in history—"Music and the Spoken Word," with the Tabernacle Choir, broadcast every Sunday since 1929, now on two thousand stations around the world. Utah has six national parks, but Temple Square attracts more people every year than any of them.

You can't go inside the Temple unless you are a Mormon and have a recommendation from your bishop, but you can go inside the wall to see the Tabernacle and the two visitor centers with movies and dioramas. The official tours are usually guided by young sister missionaries who will bear their testimony at the drop of a hat, telling you how they know Joseph Smith was a prophet of God and that the Book of Mormon is true. They glow while they say these things, light coming from a burning in their bosom, and it can be very appealing because they are genuinely happy. Pretty soon you'll be writing down your address for them. But then it will be the young brother missionaries who will come to your house. No matter where you live, they will find you, and it will be difficult to make them go away.

I will take you on my own tour of Temple Square, but I'd like to start with the white marble statue of Joseph Smith in the lobby of the old Hotel Utah, just across Main Street from Temple Square.

Built in 1911, eleven stories tall, glazed white with a beehive on top, the Hotel Utah offered the finest accommodations between Denver and San Francisco and was known as the "Grande Dame." It hosted U.S. presidents, foreign dignitaries, and Hollywood movie stars, but turned away Ella Fitzgerald and Harry Belafonte. In 1987 the Church closed the hotel and converted it to offices, a genealogy library, meeting rooms, and an IMAX theater now showing *Joseph Smith: The Prophet of the Restoration*.

The statue of Joseph Smith stands in the old hotel lobby, which was preserved for historical value. The room is ringed by grey marble pillars two stories tall with a stained-glass ceiling and an enormous crystal chandelier hanging down in the center. The statue is ten feet tall and very white—Joseph in a suit coat and bow tie, holding the Book of Mormon.

You can walk right up and stand in front of him, gazing up at his proud and handsome face. But when you look down about eye level, you see he's wearing some pretty tight pants and there's a six- or seven-inch bulge between his legs, like the back of a white whale surfacing above the water. You can touch it if you want, even rub it like in the Catholic and Hindu traditions. But I've never seen anyone actually do it and I don't know what would happen if you did.

Let's go outside and look at the Brigham Young statue. He's up there on top of a granite monolith, twenty-five feet in the air, standing over Main Street looking southward down the valley. His left arm is raised, palm up and open as if to say, "Someday, my son, all of this will be yours."

Brigham Young and Joseph Smith were both strong, charismatic leaders, but their personalities were opposite in nature, like Stalin and Lenin, and so too are their statues. Joseph is carved in white marble, immaculate, while Brigham is cast in bronze that has blackened over time. This is not to say that Brigham has lost his standing among Church historians; that's not the case at all. He was just different in nearly every way from Joseph. Joseph was a utopian visionary who led by inspiration; Brigham was pragmatic and led with a hammer.

Joseph Smith said he was visited by angels, prophets, Jesus Christ, and God Himself. He said he'd been told that all religions on Earth had fallen into apostasy and that he'd been chosen to restore the one true gospel and build a New Jerusalem in America so Jesus would have a place to come back to. Joseph and his early followers tried building the New Jerusalem in Kirtland, Ohio, then Independence, Missouri, and then Nauvoo, Illinois, but in each location they were met by opposition and persecution from their non-Mormon neighbors. Then, in June 1844, in the middle of his campaign to become president of the United States, Joseph was killed by an angry mob in Carthage, Illinois.

And it came to pass that the Saints of the Latter Days would move again and find another place to build the Kingdom of God on Earth. Joseph himself, shortly before he was killed, said he'd received a revelation that the Saints were to move to a location in the Rocky Mountains, as foretold in the book of Isaiah:

> And it shall come to pass in the last days, that the mountain of the Lord's house shall be established in the top of the mountains and shall be exalted above the hills, and all nations shall flow into it. (Isaiah 2:2)

But it was Brigham Young who brought the Saints across the Great Plains to the Great Basin in covered wagons. It was

Brigham who was tough as nails and pushed the envelope of space, moving his people outside the territory of the United States into an uncontrolled part of Mexico where they would be left alone. There were bands of Native Americans living along the western slope of the Wasatch Mountains, but the Salt Lake Valley was a no-man's-land, a buffer zone between the Shoshones to the north and the Utes to the south. Later, of course, there were massacres, small and large, but in the beginning the pioneers walked into open space—a high desert basin covered in dry grass and sage brush.

They arrived on July 24, 1847, and Brigham Young already had the map of the new city plotted out in his mind. It was to be a rational system, a Cartesian grid with the temple as the "0,0" origin point, the axes running to the cardinal directions. This earthly city would be a mirror image of the heavenly city where God and Jesus live, and it would be a gathering place where all would be of one heart and mind, the City of Zion.

For three days Brigham Young walked around, scouting out the valley, trying to decide where to put the temple. He knew that whatever spot he chose would be ground zero for time and all eternity. Finally, near the bank of a stream at the northern end of the valley, he jabbed his cane into the dirt and said, "This is where we will build a temple to our God."

It was a good decision, a nice location. From here you can watch the Wasatch mountains like a wraparound drive-in movie.

Thus did Brigham speak, and thus did the Salt Lake Valley, empty of meaning and purpose, become part of a transcendent reality—absolute. Land was transformed into property, chaos into cosmos. The x and y axes of the Cartesian grid ran to the cardinal points. The temple itself would be the third axis, the z, running straight up to heaven and down to the center of the Earth.

Brigham named all the streets and addresses in the valley from this spot. For instance, the second street to the east he called Second East, and the fourth street to the south he called Fourth South. So today wherever you go in the valley, whether as a believer or an unbeliever, your position is described as a set of coordinates in relation to the temple.

We can't go into the Temple, but we can walk right up to it, walk all the way around it, and even touch it. It is made of light grey, almost white, granite quarried from the base of Little Cottonwood Canyon, fifteen miles to the south. It took them forty years to build. They hauled the stone by oxcart and railway and cut it into perfect square blocks and stacked it up so seamlessly and straight that the building looks as if it was carved in place from one giant rock. It has six spires, the highest spire holding the gold-plated statue of the angel Moroni with his long trumpet pointed to the east—an air raid siren for the Apocalypse. They don't call themselves Saints of the "Latter Days" for nothing.

Inside the Temple the righteous enact rituals called ordinances and covenants—baptisms, endowments of the priesthood, marriages for time and all eternity, and different blessings. These are sacred ceremonies and the language and symbolisms used are not to be discussed in public. They are secrets, and even Mormons who have fallen away from the church and no longer believe its doctrines will refuse to speak of the ceremonies that go on inside because of the promises they made there with God.

I first heard about these ceremonies when I was eight years old, walking to school with my two friends. They told me they'd been baptized in the Temple and now they were going to a different heaven than I was, unless I converted. They said there are three levels of heaven and they were going to the highest one, the Celestial Kingdom, but the best I could hope for was the second level, the Terrestrial Kingdom, which isn't a bad place, just not the best place. There is, they said, no hell, except for a few really bad people, Sons of Perdition, who are cast into the Outer Darkness.

The best thing about the highest heaven, where they were going, was that through "the law of eternal progression" they would someday become gods, like our God now, with their own planet, only somewhere else in the universe. They said they were telling me all this because they didn't want me to miss out. They wanted me to start reading the Book of Mormon and praying about whether it was true. Each of us had peach fuzz on our faces and pants with patches ironed onto the knees, and we were carrying "new math" textbooks, yet they were on their way to godhood and I was just walking to second grade.

The power of the Temple is mighty and strong. Touch it. Feel the rock—nine feet thick at the base, six feet thick at the top. The foundation goes down forty feet. When I touch it I think of Lone Peak, which is the same rock, the same granite. You can stand on this rock on top of Lone Peak and look down here and see Temple Square, twenty miles away. You can see the whole valley, and then you can ski down into it. That's probably not as good as becoming a god. It's more like becoming a bird.

There are four doors to the Temple, two on the east and two on the west, but everyone enters and exits through a tunnel underground. The doors will open when Jesus comes back. Until then, they stay locked.

Since we can't go inside, we should walk around to the flagpole between the Temple and the Tabernacle, in the exact center of the square. From here you can look up and see the American flag juxtaposed against the upper spires of the Temple. This is the money shot. In Utah, church and state go together like muscle and bone, intertwined in Mormon mythology. Joseph Smith believed Jesus "raised up" our founding fathers and guided their hands in writing the Constitution in order to make a new nation, tolerant of religious beliefs, where the restoration of the gospel could come about. In other words, Mormons believe the United States of America was designed by Jesus for Joseph Smith to become God's prophet of this last chapter of civilization as we know it. The flag and the temple, the temple and the flag, in the center of the center of the cosmos, where Jesus is going to live when he comes back.

I used to resist the church. I spoke out against it whenever and wherever I had a chance. But one day a question entered my head—"What if, by a wave of my hand, I could wipe out all of Mormon history, erase the whole thing as if it never existed? Would I do it?" It took me five seconds to realize I would never do it. I'd miss their stories, their mythic value. I'd miss the Temple even though I can't go inside it, maybe especially because I can't go inside it. My identity, the person I have become, is a non-Mormon, an outsider, *other*. If the Mormons were gone, then who would I be?

So I watch the light, through the seasons, as it hits the buildings downtown, seen through the trees in my neighborhood. This is where I meet and learn about the natural and supernatural worlds. My bones are made from dry desert air; my blood is made from water that falls as snow. My cells vibrate to the sound of train horns from the bottom of the valley.

Listen: inside the Tabernacle the choir is humming. The Prophet speaks:

> The morning breaks, the shadows flee
> Lo Zion's standard is unfurled
> The dawning of a brighter day, majestic rises on the world
> Clouds of air disappear before the rays of truth divine
> Glory bursting from afar, wide o'er the nation soon will shine.

The Tabernacle is the cosmic egg that holds the sound of the universe before the big bang. The choir softly hums and the oval room becomes infinite, a nomosphere, the center where all things are true and real even if they make no sense and maybe it's all made up. It's something the Mormons can make happen like magic, and they do it very well.

I used to want to leave and never come back, but now I see I'm held here. I am the prisoner of Zion.

Ishmael
October 2001

Shortly before I left for Afghanistan, my lawyer called and said, "You may not know this, but you need to get your bail bondsman's permission in order to leave the country. Legally, he owns your body and he may not want you transporting it to a war zone."

Some weeks earlier, actually the day we started bombing Afghanistan, October 7, 2001, Columbus Day weekend, I was arrested and thrown in jail—not for protesting the war, but over some trouble we were having in my neighborhood.

I'd been at work and when I came home, my wife said, "One of those guys from around the corner was here again. He came in the house and wouldn't leave. He had a cast on his leg and he said he had to go out to his grandmother's house in Murray and he had to take a cab because his leg was broken. He wanted twenty bucks and I said no but he wouldn't leave so I just gave him the money."

There was a house of junkies just around the corner. I'd seen them on the street, smoking, waiting for the bus, shivering, impatient. I've got nothing against drug addicts—so many of us are—but they were bad drug addicts. From the time they arrived in the neighborhood, my car had been broken into, my tools stolen from the garage, and my wife and kids "visited" and hit up for money on three occasions. That's inappropriate behavior, scaring the wife and kids. They were bad people and I decided, maybe like dropping a bomb, to just go over there and walk into their house without knocking. Which I did.

There were two guys and a woman in the living room, a guy throwing up in the bathroom, and another guy in a bedroom throwing clothes, frantically looking for something before bolting out the glass door. I told the three in the living room to sit down, that we were going to have a talk. I said, "You're not going to come over to my house anymore," but they were all yelling at me and trying to leave and I wouldn't let them. One guy came at me with a pair of handcuffs and I grabbed them and pushed him back and he fell to the floor. "That's it," he said, "you just lost your house. That's assault, and I have emphysema, and I'm going to sue you for everything you're worth."

He grabbed the phone and called 9-1-1 and then I took the phone from him and talked to the dispatcher. I told her I was "holding" some people who had scared my wife and kids and I wanted the police to come over and arrest them. The dispatcher wanted to know details—Who was I? Who were they? They were all yelling and trying to leave, and it was hard to explain. She tried to keep me on phone, but I hung up.

After forty-five minutes two young female officers arrived, wearing new uniforms and shiny badges. I told them what happened, but I think perhaps they lacked the necessary field experience to pick through the social complexities of the situation, and they ended up taking me to jail for burglary (a felony), unlawful detention, and assault. Bail was set at $12,000, which meant we had to put up $1,200 and a lien on our house, and, since it was Columbus Day weekend, I had to sit in jail for a couple of days, long enough to contemplate my enigma.

I'd already decided to go to Afghanistan. On 9/11 I saw the future—a religious war that would ruin everything, bring it down like the Apocalypse, and a few days later I applied for a visa to Uzbekistan. I thought I could get into Afghanistan from the north, the way the Soviets went in.

What I thought about in jail were the bars in front of me. Of course I should have called the police and filed a complaint instead of going over to the house. I had taken the law into my own hands and now I was locked in jail with criminals, cells stacked three stories high in a semicircle so that one guard, a woman, could sit at an elevated control panel in the center of the circle and see into every cell. I could also see every other cell, except for those right below me, and I was the only prisoner standing with his hands on the bars looking out. I took solace knowing I was also the only prisoner with a visa to Uzbekistan.

So, anyway, two weeks before I left for Afghanistan I had to go down to Beehive Bail Bonds, across the street from the library, to talk to the man who owned my body. He was an older man, my father's age. He clasped his hands together and set them down on the desk in front of him and said, "I've been in this business for a long time and have seen many strange things, but your case is new to me. I wanted to meet you, face-to-face, because I think you might have a screw loose."

"Okay," I said, "fire away."

"First," he said, "I should let you know that I've talked to the police and charges are not going to be brought on this one. It turns out your neighbor across the street is a prosecutor for the county. Did you know that?"

"No," I said, "I didn't. I knew he's a lawyer. But I didn't know he works for the county."

"Yes, he does and he prosecutes the felony cases, so he would have been the one bringing you to trial, but it turns out these same people that you burglarized, assaulted, and illegally detained had been in his home several times scaring his wife and kids as well. They'd been going door-to-door all over your neighborhood. So there's not going to be a trial. You're a lucky man, considering what a stupid thing you did. They could have had a gun."

"Junkies don't have guns," I said. "They pawn them."

He stared at me for a second or two, leaned back in his chair, set his clasped hands upon his stomach, and said, "So, why do you want to go to Afghanistan?"

"It's my job," I said.

"Who do you work for?"

"I'm an independent writer and radio producer. I do the stories and then sell them, mainly to men's magazines you don't read and public radio programs you've never heard of."

"So you don't really have a job. You're self-employed. Nobody is sending you over there."

"That's correct," I said. "Sometimes I have a contract and expense money, but not this time. Which reminds me, if the charges are dropped, do I get back the $1,200?"

"No," he said. "I keep the $1,200, and you didn't answer my question. Why do you want to do this? You could write about something else instead."

"After the attacks," I said, "what else is there?"

"Let someone else go."

"I don't trust anyone else." I was certain of that. "I don't believe the news. The news is selling this war and we're buying it. We're the richest nation on the planet and Afghanistan is the poorest nation on the planet. It's not war, it's a business, a trap, and we're walking right into it."

"You don't think we can win?" he asked with nearly a guffaw, which got me pissed.

"How do you hit something you can't see?" I jabbed back. "Our enemy is called Al Qaeda, which means 'the base,' but it's not a physical base like a fortress, it's the spiritual base of their beliefs. We think the problem is physical—we'll just go over there and kill the bad guys—but the problem is not physical. It's spiritual. Because of this, when we attack them, we only make them stronger. Look at early Mormon history. Every time they were persecuted or attacked, it only made them stronger."

"But these guys *did* attack us. How do you stop them from doing it again?"

"It's their decision. If they want to attack us, they can and will. The only way to stop them is to make it so they don't want to do it in the first place. To do that, we at least need to know who they are. I'm going to go find out."

"You ever consider you might be doing the same thing as your neighbors, scaring your wife and kids?" He was getting mean.

"But they're not scared," I said. "I've been to war zones and dangerous places before. I always come back."

"I imagine they worry anyway."

I couldn't answer. He ate me like a sack lunch.

"Well," he said, "the police haven't finished the paperwork, and until they do you're technically not supposed to leave the country, but as far as I'm concerned you can go, even though I still think you might have a screw loose."

Over There:
Afghanistan After the Fall
Late November 2001

I hand my passport to a man in a military uniform at the port of Termez, Uzbekistan. A few feet away is the Oxus, the river that serves as the border with Afghanistan, running fast and full of glacial silt. The officer's hat rises steeply in front to support a large golden badge, and from his shoulders hang golden epaulets. His boots come up to his knees. I'm shaking in my shoes and would not be surprised if he pointed to my Afghan visa and shook his head—"No, it is not possible." I'm amazed to have an Afghan visa, amazed to be standing next to the Oxus River, and I have nagging suspicions there are reasons why this is not allowed. But the officer sets my passport down on a table and takes out his stamp and presses it onto the page, signs it, and then hands it back to me.

The river is deep enough for tugboats to push barges to the other side, and there are barges tied to the dock being loaded with bags of rice and wheat from the United Nations. Since

1996, there's been a severe drought in northern Afghanistan. Then, in 1998, the Taliban took control, sending the country back to the days of Mohammed. A lot of people in Afghanistan are starving, or so I read in the papers.

I've never been to Afghanistan and know very little about it. I was in Kashmir in 1998 and can clearly remember the angry looks from Muslim men—not all of them, just those who wanted Kashmir to be an independent Muslim state. They saw me, an American, as their enemy and they didn't hide their emotions: they wanted to kill me. I thought their anger was misplaced because they were fighting India, not the United States. An Indian captain stationed on the Line of Control with Pakistan told me many of the insurgents his men were killing were not Kashmiri but Afghani, trained in camps and sent to fight the holy war in Kashmir. I should have listened more carefully. I should have gone to Afghanistan back then.

I get on a tugboat with four other journalists and we start across the river, heading straight into the current. It's strong and bites into the bow and the captain pushes down on the throttle. For the first time in weeks, I relax. I breathe deeply. The water smells like cold glacial mud. I feel the line being crossed and yes, I want to go. I was afraid I wouldn't get in, afraid I'd have to stay home and watch the war on television and listen to everybody say "God is on our side." My guess is that God won't have anything to do with it. My guess is God doesn't care one way or the other. There's that, and also maybe I don't want to live anymore . . . but it feels pretty good right now.

On the shore of Afghanistan a man in a worn-out sport coat and scarf stamps my passport, no problem, and I cram into an already full Toyota microbus going to Mazar-i-Sharif, sixty miles to the south. We drive on a ribbon of asphalt across sand dunes and drifted snow, the middle of Asia, empty except for some nomads with a Bactrian double-hump camel and an Afghan hound—like a cross between a mastiff and a Newfoundland.

As we approach the city the road is lined with metal shipping containers, all left behind by the Soviets. Now people are living inside them—a rusted-steel-cube shantytown on top of a garbage heap, plastic bags blowing in the wind as we drive by. The women are covered in burkhas; the men wear long shirts and pajama pants held up by a string around the waist. They wrap blankets around their shoulders but they have no socks and their shoes are plastic slippers.

Mazar-i-Sharif sits on the flatlands before the northern slope of the Hindu Kush. The foothills are ten miles away. Beyond the foothills the mountains rise up like the teeth of a wood rasp, fifteen thousand feet tall and covered in snow, impenetrable. The streets of Mazar are mud and the buildings are brick-and-concrete cubes, side-by-side, flat rooftops with clusters of rebar sticking up like wild grass. I'm dropped off at the hotel, the one hotel that's open, just across the street from a blue-tiled mosque. All the journalists are staying here, from all over Europe and Japan.

My room is tiny and cold—four walls, a window, and a thin cotton mattress on top of wire springs that sag and creak almost to the floor when I lie down on them. The electricity is off. The bathroom is down the hall but I'm told there is no water now. There's a restaurant, but it's not open. I stare at a bare lightbulb hanging from the ceiling as the noonday call to prayer breaks through a loudspeaker at the mosque. It's not a recording. It's an actual guy over there in the minaret and he's wailing a song that's more than one thousand years old. It's beautiful, soul-wrenching, and frightening.

I decide to go for a walk. I leave the hotel, cross the street to the mosque, the blue-tiled dome, and stop there to look at it. The instant I stop walking, four or five young men also stop walking, as if they'd just been pretending to be going somewhere. They stand right in front me. Then quickly there are ten, then thirty—all boys and men, crowding close together, a hundred eyes looking at me as if they can't believe what they are seeing.

"Where are you from?" a teenage boy asks.

"America," I say, wondering if this is a good thing because we'd just bombed their city and their country. But it's the word they want to hear; they want to say it. *America . . . America . . . America . . .*

"California," I say, wanting to hear it echo. "Mississippi."

Three or four of them are trying to speak English.

"Hello, how are you?"

"Thank you very much."

"Okay, good luck, good-bye."

"What do you think about America bombing your country?" I ask the teenager. "Was it a good thing or a bad thing?"

"It was a good thing. The Taliban . . . the Taliban . . . when the Taliban here there was no working, nothing working. Now America comes here. Is it correct? America comes here?"

"You mean will American soldiers come here? I don't know, maybe."

The boy translates this for the crowd and they start shouting questions, too many to translate. Sort of frustrated, he says, "We want money to make work. We want now the schools."

"I think there might be some money," I say, "but I don't know, we might start bombing some other country and forget about Afghanistan."

This makes the yelling get louder. They're not yelling at me, but more just yelling for the sake of yelling, filling the space with their voices. I look down and there's a guy in a small cart like a wheelchair. One of his legs is missing and the other is very short, like a baby's. He's saying he needs a new cart, a real wheelchair with bicycle tires like they make in America, and some artificial limbs like they make in America, and he wants to know if I can get him some.

"I don't know how to do that," I say, "but it's possible. I think that's one of the things there will be money for."

They just keep pressing in, getting tighter and tighter, and I'm feeling like it's time to start saying whatever they want to hear, like it's time to get going. So I say, "Okay. Good luck. Good-bye," and wave and walk with intention through the crowd, quickly back across the street, and into the hotel.

I climb six floors to the roof of the hotel and look at the mosque, which from here looks like an elaborate piece of turquoise jewelry surrounded by trees and walkways. The inner dome is said to hold the tomb of Ali, the cousin and son-in-law of the Prophet Mohammed and the fourth Caliph of Islam. Nothing else in the city even comes close to its beauty. There are men in the street pulling carts with wooden wheels; other carts are pulled by horses and donkeys, carrying wood and bricks. There are shops with skinned goats hanging upside-down out front, shops where chairs and tables are made, shops with material for clothing and drapes. If you took away the cars and the shop where the guy is making satellite dishes from pieces of scrap metal, and ignored the occasional Soviet-made proletarian concrete building, then the city would look like it had been built in the thirteenth century, or even earlier.

Again I go out for a walk, and again I stop, and again four or five men around me immediately also stop. They'd been acting as if they were going on their way, but really they were just wandering about without enough purpose to propel them beyond my stopping. And again a crowd quickly forms around me. This time I pull out my camera and start taking pictures. They become quiet and still—not afraid or shy of the camera, but also not quite sure of its power. I hold it at arm's length down low and they stare straight at the lens and I take their pictures. While I'm doing this I hear a voice, a soft, calm voice next to my ear say, "Excuse me, are you a journalist?" I turn and see a young man with a shaved head.

"Sort of," I say.

He's wearing a Planet Hollywood T-shirt over a brown turtleneck, checked polyester pants two or three sizes too big and cinched by a belt—and I have a feeling he might actually be a girl. He has beautiful eyes with long lashes, and a soft voice.

"What are you doing?" he asks.

"Just taking pictures," I say. "How old are you?"

"Nineteen. Do you need a translator? I have been studying English in school, but there is no school now—the Taliban sent our teachers back to Turkey. I would very much like to work for you. I will help you in any way that I can, and I will not leave your side—as long as you are here I will be with you."

"What's your name?"

"Najibullah."

"Najibullah, why did you shave your head?"

"When the Taliban leave two weeks ago many men shave their beard, but I do not have beard, so I shave my hair," he says, smiling.

"Good one," I say, "but I'm sorry, I don't have very much money, and I just can't afford to pay a translator every day."

"For me money is not important. If you have money, you can pay me. If you don't have money, you don't pay me. When you are finished you can decide."

I know this is a deal that could go sour very quickly, but I do need a translator and, to a certain degree, I believe him. He's trying to learn to look and act like a Westerner, and probably the best way for him to do it would be to hang out with me. I wonder if his shaved head might frighten the locals, but, then, he is a local and it's his business so I let it go.

"Come," he says, "let's go to the hotel and we can talk there."

We've attracted a large crowd, some of them spilling into the street, making traffic go around them.

"This place is not so good for you."

We walk through the crowd and they go on about their business, all except for three very dirty little boys who try to stand in front of me and brush my hand begging for money, but all I have are $20 bills. Najibullah saves me by scolding them and making them go away.

Nighttime

Only two weeks ago, the Taliban controlled Mazar-i-Sharif and all of northern Afghanistan. They hid in the city, among civilians, where the United States would be afraid to bomb them. But we bombed them anyway with precision strikes— on a girl's school where they were sleeping and at the airport, where we neatly snuffed out all their leftover MiG fighter jets. And then the Northern Alliance began to surround the city. The Taliban were mainly Pashtun, the Northern Alliance mainly Uzbek and Tajik, and they had fought two wars in this city already, killing thousands both times. So the Taliban, under threat of being trapped, fled the city in pickups and trucks—east toward Pakistan, and south to Kabul and on to Kandahar. Some, perhaps as many as ten thousand, stopped in Kunduz, a hundred miles east of here. There they were bombed from the air by American planes, surrounded on the ground by the Northern Alliance, and forced to surrender. Last week, about four hundred and fifty Taliban surrendered just outside Mazar-i-Sharif. They were taken to a fortress on the other side of the city, where they were held overnight. In the morning, they started an uprising, killing an American CIA agent who had come to interrogate them. They took control of the fortress. A three-day-long battle ensued with heavy bombing from the air, artillery from the ground, and a lot of shooting. But it's over now. All the Taliban were killed, except for a few who are still hiding out in "a bunker" and refuse to surrender.

This all happened before I got here.

Morning

I ask Najibullah if we can get a car and go to Sheberghan, a town a hundred miles to the west, where there's a prison full of captured Taliban. I want to interview them. He leaves and comes back in half an hour with a ten-year-old Corolla and a driver.

Yesterday Najibullah told me that *Titanic* was such a hit in Mazar that now if you want to say that someone is "with the latest style" you say that he is Titanic. I tell Najibullah that he is Titanic. I loaned him my sunglasses and hat, and he thinks he looks like a U.S. Special Forces soldier. He says that other people can't tell he's an Afghan, and this makes him very happy.

He's driving the car—the old chauffeur relaxing in the passenger seat, willing to let the nineteen-year-old go ninety miles an hour across the desert—pounding the steering wheel to the beat of some Afghan disco music. He drives too fast, and he slows down and speeds up too quickly. They drive on the right side of the road in Afghanistan, but the cars are from Pakistan and the steering wheel is on the right side. This is a problem when Najib is passing big trucks without slowing down, so the old chauffeur helps him out by saying whether it's clear.

Always, when passing, Najibullah blows his horn for the entire distance. Everybody does. There are many potholes in the asphalt, some that can be avoided without slowing down, but others that quickly go from bad to worse. Najibullah slams on the brakes as the car crashes through a series of large holes. This happens again and again, even though I keep telling him to slow down.

The first few miles of the trip are across farmland. We pass through three fortress-size walls. They're about twenty-five feet high and spaced two to three miles apart, and they run in a straight line across open land. At two of the walls there are gates with checkpoints where young men with Kalashnikovs and walkie-talkies come up to look in the car. Najibullah speaks to them in English, trying out that Special Forces thing, and when they hear the words *journalist* and *American* they back off and wave us through.

The land looks like it's been lying fallow for years. The fields are bordered by trees, and every few miles there's a small village, the houses made from adobe, all having the shape of a cube topped by a dome. Najibullah tells me these people are Hazaras, Shia Muslims, from Iran.

Fifteen miles northwest of Mazar is the ancient city of Balkh, the so-called mother of all cities, where there are more walls and fortresses. Back in the days of the silk trade, the road between the Middle East and China went through here, as did the road from Kabul and Delhi going north into the 'stans and Russia. Balkh was a crossroads and the capital of ancient Bactria, sacked by Alexander and the Mongols, and home of the poet Rumi. Some of the walls now have nearly completely eroded back into the ground, but others are in good condition. Where the highway forks to go into the city, there's a huge man-made mound—fifty feet tall and one hundred and fifty feet wide, with a Soviet-era tank parked on top, the highest lookout point.

Beyond Balkh the farms and fortresses stop and the desert takes over. In the distance there are small caravans of camels and herds of goats, and running along next to the road is a natural gas pipeline, rusted, resting on the ground or on small dirt mounds spaced one hundred yards apart.

"Is that a real pipeline?" I ask Najibullah.

"Yes, it's real. It's the only one in Afghanistan. Built by the Russians. The gas comes from the ground near Sheberghan and goes to Mazar."

"And it actually works?"

"Yes, for electricity in Mazar. We have one five-megawatt station. My father, he helped in building this, as geology engineer."

Up ahead there's a teenage boy with a Kalashnikov on the side of the road, and Najibullah pulls over and stops. It's not a checkpoint—he just wants a ride, and we have to stop because he has a gun. This is a common form of transportation for the soldiers, but when the kid comes up to the car, the old chauffeur starts yelling at him in Farsi, "What are you doing? You shouldn't be out here stopping cars on the highway. This man is an American and you should be careful not to upset him or the bombs will find you in your house!" The kid falls back like he's been punched hard.

"He really believed that," I say as we pull away.

"Yes, they all believe it," Najibullah says. "And it's true."

"Yeah, but I can't make it happen."

"But he does not know this."

The old man looks at me and smiles.

In Sheberghan we stop at the compound of General Abdul Rashid Dostum. He's one of the leaders of the Northern Alliance and Sheberghan is his home base. If we want to talk to the Taliban at the prison, we need to get his permission.

Dostum's compound takes up a full city block, surrounded by a white wall. The doors at the gate are heavy metal, big enough for tanks. Inside there are two swimming pools—one indoors and one outdoors, both empty and breaking apart.

Dostum's house, modest for a war/druglord, is in the center of the compound. Some of our special forces are staying there, maybe six, maybe Delta Force soldiers working for the State Department or the CIA. They were some of the first troops into the country, and they've been working with Dostum since they got here.

Beyond the house is a garden with long rows of rose bushes and fruit trees, sidewalks and benches, a small mosque in one corner, and a large concrete fountain in the shape of an opium poppy, also out of order.

The biggest building in the compound is the guesthouse, which is like a hotel where the paintings in the lobby are scenes from the Garden of Eden, but the heads of the animals have been cut out, leaving square holes in the canvas. Only a couple of weeks ago, the Taliban lived here and Dostum was in exile in Uzbekistan. Now he's back, but the heads of the animals in the paintings are lost forever.

There's a long conference room on the third floor where Dostum is meeting with more than one hundred local mullahs and commanders. The room is remarkable in that it's clean and has new red carpet and black felt drapes, chandeliers hanging from the ceiling, new couches and upholstered chairs, and a forty-eight-inch flat-screen television with a satellite connection.

The men are sitting in the chairs and cross-legged on the floor, wearing turbans on their heads and blankets wrapped around their shoulders, older men with grey beards, all ethnic Uzbeks. For three years they've been in hiding in the mountains.

Dostum is dressed in velour like a medieval monarch— a big man with a round face, woolly caterpillar eyebrows, salt-and-pepper hair, his beard trimmed short and neat. A teddy bear, but also a powerful warlord who is reportedly so strong he has crushed a man's skull with his bare hands, and so cruel that he is said to have tied a man to the treads of a tank and then personally smooshed him into the ground. He may look huggable, but he is a very dangerous man. He sided with the Soviets during the 1980s and built his army by running drugs. During the 1990s, when Afghanistan was torn by civil war, he sided with everyone and no one, making and breaking many promises.

One of the mullahs stands and tells Dostum that his office in a nearby town has no furniture or carpets left, that the Taliban took everything.

"Here you have new things," he says, "but we have nothing left, not even a desk."

Dostum takes this in stride and tells the man that these things will not be a problem, but that they will take some time. He has only just now arrived in town.

A younger man, a commander, stands and tells Dostum that there are still Taliban soldiers hiding in bunkers outside his village and that they've threatened to die fighting before they surrender. Dostum tells him to tell the Taliban they must surrender or they will be bombed by U.S. planes until there will be none of them left.

A man walks to the center of the room holding a sheet of paper in his shaking hands. He stands there and looks at the paper and then he starts to sing. It's a dirge with many verses, telling of battles where brothers and friends fought bravely but were lost. All the men in the room know the stories because they were there when it happened, and some of them are sobbing, tears falling onto the blankets around their chests. They don't want to fight anymore—not because they are afraid of fighting, but because they are really very tired of fighting.

After the meeting I'm told that General Dostum isn't seeing anyone else today, so we go back to Mazar-i-Sharif.

Nighttime

The power is off in the hotel as well as the entire city of Mazar, but I have a headlamp and a box of wooden matches. The headlamp I brought with me, but the matchbox is from Latvia, and I can't remember how it came to me. Maybe by way of the *Boston Globe* reporter from Moscow on the fifth floor of the hotel. They are fine wooden matches, "Avion," with a picture of an old airplane. The box is also made of wood, and sturdy. It seems very exotic and very much out of place.

There is no power or running water in this hotel, and I've been waiting for an hour for dinner to be brought to my room. I asked the ten-year-old concierge if there was a way I could order something to eat. He speaks English pretty well, although sometimes with an attitude, but we get along because I tip him 10,000 Afghani soom (30 cents) whenever he does something for me.

"Yes," he snaps, "what do you want?"

"Do you have dinner?" I inquire.

"Dinner?" he says, as if he'd never heard the word.

"Yes, dinner, like kabob. Do you have kabob?"

"Kabob, no."

"Rice?"

"Yes, rice."

"And bread?"

"Rice and bread."

"And tea."

"Okay."

"Do you have anything else?"

"What?"

"Is there anything else they can make in the kitchen besides rice and bread and tea?"

"No."

"Okay then. Can you bring it to my room?"

"Yes, yes."

And he went off into the darkness and he has not come back. But there are many hungry people in this town. I roll another cigarette and light it with my exotic matches and listen to the last prayer of the day blaring enormous from the loudspeaker at the mosque.

Morning

I am standing outside the Ministry of Foreign Affairs waiting for the young Najibullah to tell the authorities of our plans. I want to go to Qala-i-Jhangi, the scene of the battle I missed. Najibullah must report in and ask for permission to go, he says, or they will get rough with him. So I wait. Next to me is a Toyota Tacoma four-door, four-wheel-drive pickup with a diesel engine and the steering wheel on the right side. It has chrome bars over the front grill and chrome running boards. In the bed there are three soldiers. The one in the middle is straddling a floor-mounted machine gun with a bore the size of three fingers. The man to his left cradles a medium-size machine gun with fold-down tripod so that it can be set on the ground or maybe a rock. The other soldier has a Kalashnikov over his shoulder. They're waiting for their commander, who has also gone inside the building.

The sun is out, but it's a cold morning and two of the soldiers are wearing flight uniforms dropped from American planes as part of the humanitarian aid program—thick insulated pants, big coats with fur-lined hoods, and black leather lace-up combat boots. It would be really cold riding in the back of a pickup and these clothes are perfect for the job, so they're styling, maybe Titanic. It's cool to sit in the back of a pickup with a machine gun. It's cool to be part of the conquering army on a bright and sunny morning.

I look inside the cab and the floors and seats are covered with Afghan carpets that look like they've just been vacuumed. There's no mud or dirt anywhere, which seems impossible considering it's been raining for days and there's mud everywhere. On the dashboard there are red plastic roses, and the front window has little multicolored cotton balls hanging from its border. There are stickers of valentine hearts around the cassette player and the word LOVE written in a 1960s psychedelic font.

I point to the stickers and look at the soldiers and one of them says, "Taliban."

"Taliban?" I ask.

"Yes," he says and makes a motion with his hand meaning that the truck had belonged to the Taliban. I have the same kind of truck back home, although it's a few years newer. My cab usually has empty beer cans under the seat, and I don't have any stickers or flowers. Mine is a workhorse and this is a warhorse, the warhorse of the enemy of the guys who are now driving it. It's strange they didn't get rid of the decorations, that they chose not to change the Taliban styling. The Taliban, to these guys, must be very hip and cool.

Najibullah comes back exasperated and says we can't go to Qala-i-Jhangi.

"The Minister of Foreign Affairs is not allowing anyone to go today," he says. "There is still too much water in the basement."

"What?" I ask.

"There are dead bodies in the basement, and they can't get them out because they are floating in water."

"So why can't we go to Qala-i-Jhangi?" I still don't understand.

"This is what the Minister of Foreign Affairs tells me, and I can't argue with him," says Najib, at the end of his rope. "Everyone must wait a couple of days for the water to go into the ground."

Nighttime

I've been cold at night, so before going to bed I ask for an extra blanket. I find the young man who sweeps the floors and say, "Blanket?" making the motions like I'm sleeping and pulling a blanket over my head.

"Blanket?" he asks.

"Yeah, blanket," I reply, acting like I'm in bed and shivering.

"Okay, blanket," he says and goes directly to a room just across the hall from mine and pounds on the door. The young man who answers also works in the hotel, also sweeping the floors. My guy tells him I need his blanket, so hand it over, since I'm a paying guest and all. But the other guy says no way, Jose, it's cold out tonight. My guy says, listen, you've got to give him your blanket, if you get cold you can go sleep with your friend downstairs. This makes the other guy mad and he grabs my guy at the shoulders and they start wrestling, pushing each other in and out of the room, yelling, knocking stuff over while I'm saying, "I don't want his blanket. Stop! Listen, there must be another blanket in this hotel somewhere."

They stop wrestling and just yell at each other for a few minutes, and then they're not yelling at all but talking quietly, and then they're hugging each other in the doorway and holding hands.

"Blanket?" I say, rather perturbed.

No, they both shake their heads, no.

Morning

I'm in the basement at Qala-i-Jhangi pointing my headlamp at the bodies of Taliban soldiers lying half-buried in rust-colored mud. They've been dead for days, floating in water, but now the water has gone down and the mud floor is swallowing the bodies, swallowing my feet up to my shins, making a loud, sucking sound when I walk. The smell burns the skin on the inside of my nose. They'll never get the bodies out of here. They'd have to dig them up and then rebury them.

I'm watching a man, a worker, carry wet coats up the stairs from the basement. He carries them on his shoulder, carefully avoiding an unexploded mortar sticking out of the wall. They will search the pockets and then sell the coats to poor people who are so cold they don't mind wearing something that smells of death.

I'm sitting outside the building, using a stick to pick the mud off my boots. It's not working because the mud is like cement. There are three inches of snow on the ground and it's snowing, lightly. There are bricks lying everywhere from exploded walls, and at first I don't notice that the brick next to me is not a brick at all but a human foot broken off at the shin. It's charred and swollen, with a tuft of snow on the heel. I look at the foot and go back to cleaning my boots.

The whole thing started on November 24, a Saturday. Four hundred Taliban surrendered at dawn by simply sitting down in the desert, five miles north of Mazar-i-Sharif. They were all foreign Taliban, meaning they had come from other countries to fight the jihad, or holy war, against the Great Satan of America.

General Dostum and his militia were suspicious, and rightly so. Some of the Taliban were hiding bombs under their black tunics. For some reason, Dostum's men did not search the prisoners but simply loaded the Taliban on trucks and drove them around the city and ten miles out into the farmland, where there's a medieval-style fortress known as Qala-i-Jhangi (Fortress of War), now under the control of General Dostum.

The wall at the entrance to the fortress is sixty feet high and four hundred yards long and laced by crenellations with gunport. The gate is metal and wide enough for an elephant or a tank to fit through. Inside are farmland and pastures, maybe forty acres, with pine trees and poplars—there's a good well here.

The prisoners were taken to an area used as a pasture for Dostum's forty cavalry horses. In the middle of the pasture sits a brick building that had been used as a military school, built by the Soviets, with an air raid shelter in the basement and thick concrete walls.

The plan was to tie the prisoners' arms and then put them in the basement. However, before they could do this, one of the prisoners blew himself up, along with two high-ranking Northern Alliance commanders. Everybody hit the ground, and, to their credit, the other Northern Alliance guards did not start shooting. They pulled out and left the prisoners there for the night.

During the night, in a classroom of the school, eight of the Taliban blew themselves up. The next morning, even though the prisoners had bombs, two CIA men, "Dave" and "Mike," and two Red Cross directors, one from England and one from France, went into the compound. The Red Cross staff were there to ensure the humane treatment of the prisoners, but the CIA agents were there to interrogate them.

It's not clear what happened—either a prisoner rushed and grabbed Mike in a bear hug and blew both of them up, or threw a grenade that killed a bunch of guards, or threw a rock at a guard, knocking him down and taking his gun and killing him and five others. But something happened, and very quickly Mike was dead and Dave was running for cover. Prisoners were shooting machine guns. The guards fled the compound, shutting the gate behind them, leaving Dave and the two Red Cross directors inside.

The three white guys and their associates found a way over the outer wall of the fortress, while the Taliban found a huge cache of weapons and ammunition stored in a room near the stables. Why the prisoners had been put in an area with an arsenal of weapons was not clear. Some believed that the whole thing was a setup by the Northern Alliance. Others, including the commanding officer of the Northern Alliance, said that they believed the prisoners could be contained in the basement and that they didn't expect an uprising. But that's what happened.

For the next two days there was intense fighting on the ground, with the Taliban hiding behind trees and buildings, climbing trees to shoot over the walls of the compound, firing rockets and mortars, screaming "God is great" and running into open fire and dying, or being obliterated by bombs dropped from B-52s and artillery barrages from AC-130 gunships.

On Wednesday morning it seemed all the Taliban were dead, and the Red Cross was allowed into the compound to retrieve and bury the bodies. They found the bodies of 181 Taliban and 27 horses, many of both in pieces.

Because there were only 181 bodies in the pasture, it meant there were about 250 Taliban down in the basement, the bomb shelter of the school. Maybe they were alive; maybe they were dead. Nobody wanted to go down there and check it out.

On Thursday some old men from the street department in Mazar-i-Sharif were ordered to go down in the basement and start pulling out the bodies, but as they started down the stairs they were met by a barrage of bullets. One died, and one was wounded.

There were Taliban in the basement and they refused to surrender. They survived by coming up at night and cutting flesh off the bodies of the horses. So, first, the Northern Alliance poured gasoline and diesel fuel in the basement through a ventilation duct, and then they lit the mixture. This killed half of the prisoners.

The next day the Northern Alliance dropped rockets and hand grenades into the basement, one after another, all afternoon, so many it became monotonous and boring. This killed another half of those remaining. Still, the survivors would not surrender.

So Dostum's men flooded the basement with water, cold water from a deep well. They poured in so much water the dead bodies started floating, and men who were too injured to stand up drowned.

This was too much for those who were still alive. They began screaming for the Northern Alliance to stop, and then they started coming out, one at a time, until there were eight-six of them—wounded, wet, filthy; some had lost their minds. It was Saturday afternoon, one week after they had been brought to the fortress.

Some were treated by the Red Cross, some were given apples and oranges, all were loaded either into an open flatbed or an enclosed container to be trucked to the prison in Sheberghan. This is when a correspondent for *Newsweek* magazine, Colin Soloway, discovered that one of the prisoners was an American. He was sitting up, leaning on the tailgate of the open truck. His long black hair and beard were caked with dirt and blood, and the skin on his face was dark from soot. Soloway asked him where he was from and he said, "I was born in Washington, D.C." His name was John Walker Lindh. Now it is snowing and I am trying to clean the mud off my shoes. The pasture is pocked with bomb craters; the trunks and limbs of the pine trees are splintered to toothpicks from being ripped apart by missiles. The smell of death comes wafting up the stairway and rises through the air and the falling snow does nothing to diminish it. Najibullah is in the taxicab, honking the horn. He wants to get out of here.

Nighttime

The power is out, again, and there are eight of us in the room of the French television producer. She has three kerosene lamps and keeps her stove so hot it glows red. She has pâté, and she has vodka, and she has a satellite phone that sits on the floor and is open to anyone who needs to use it. There's a knock on the door and she yells, "Come in; don't bother to knock. Ah, Damien, you are so beautiful, I was looking for you. Please, take off your shoes."

Damien is an independent cameraman, also French, who's been trying to leave Afghanistan but has no visa to get out because he had no visa to get in. I'm not sure why. The question isn't asked.

"Damien," she says, "have some pâté. It's very good. I wanted to tell you we were at the airport today when the French troops arrived, and as it happens I know their commander. He's a very good friend of mine. We were together, years ago, in Algeria. Anyway, I mentioned there were some of us who had no way to get home and he offered to let us travel on his planes directly to Paris. What do you think of that?"

"Wonderful," he says. "You've solved all my problems and given me pâté."

Najibullah is sitting next to me on the floor, transfixed, soaking in everything. This is what he lives for, to hang out with Westerners and study their ways. He knows everyone and they all like him because he's usually happy and curious and eager to help. He's been offered other jobs for more money than I am paying him, but he's refused because of his promise to me.

There's another knock on the door and it's another Najibullah, the number-one translator in town. He's an English teacher and he wears a wool suit with a tie, a little formal and stiff for this crowd. Our host shouts out, "Come in, come in, and close the door—it's so cold in here."

He closes the door and takes off his scarf and hat and says, "I have news. The Black Priest Dadullah, he is in Baaaaalllllkhhhh." He has a way of torching the last words of certain sentences, either for emphasis or because of a speech impediment. It's hard to tell. The Taliban mullah Dadullah is in the ancient city of Balkh, the "mother of all cities," only fifteen miles away, and this means there could be trouble.

There are somewhere between two hundred and three thousand Taliban in Balkh who refuse to surrender. Or perhaps there are no Taliban there at all. It's hard to tell. The Black Priest is a hard-line Taliban leader known for his severe punishments. He swore never to surrender, but then he vanished. It was thought he was in Kandahar or that he was dead, but now he's back—or maybe he isn't.

Every day for the past week, at least one hundred and fifty of Dostum's soldiers have been in Balkh. They have three tanks and a couple dozen pickup trucks with large guns and rockets. We've been going through there, going back and forth to Sheberghan, and a commander there told me they were "cleaning up," going from house to house, disarming the occupants and looking for Taliban soldiers. I asked him if I could observe the operation, but he said they only do it at night, and so it would not be possible.

A correspondent for National Public Radio, Steve Inskeep, went to Balkh a couple of days later and asked to see the confiscated weapons and the men who had been taken prisoner, but he was given a long runaround and told there were no guns or prisoners to be seen. We were passing through Balkh on the same day and were stopped on the road about a mile outside the city because a Toyota van had been hit by a rocket-powered grenade and three men had been wounded. One guy had been taken to the hospital in Mazar; another was hit in the foot and was standing outside the van with a crutch, bleeding on the road; and the third guy was in the van with a bandage wrapped around his head, in shock. They got hit as they were passing through the edge of town, and the driver just kept going for about a mile and then stopped to figure out what just happened. They were not Taliban. It had been a mistake, caused by someone wearing the wrong color of turban.

This is the kind of slim evidence available about what's going on in Balkh. There are also rumors of looting and abductions of young women. Someone, one of us, needs to go to Balkh and find some facts, but this would be very dangerous, especially for the interpreters, and there are no volunteers. We sit in silence, looking at the kerosene lanterns, wondering if maybe there's still some more vodka.

A Trip to the Capital City

I'm running out of money. I'm spending about $80 a day, and at this rate I'll have to leave in a week, when I'm down to $200. I'll need at least that much to get across the river and back to the airport in Tashkent. So I'm running out of time but I want to go to Kabul, just to see what it's like. Also, to get to Kabul from Mazar-i-Sharif, you have to go up and over the Hindu Kush, and I very much want to see these mountains. *Hindu Kush* means "Killer of Hindus," but this terrain also killed the Greeks, the British, and the Soviets. The Afghans are very proud of their courage in standing up to foreign invaders, but their mountains, I believe, had an equal share in their victories. I want to see what it's like to travel up and over these mountains, so I ask Najibullah how much it will cost to get to Kabul and get back.

"By private car it will take $200, maybe $400."

"That's like a year's wages," I say. "There's got to be a cheaper way or no one would ever go."

"Yes, there are local cars, like taxis, and for this it is only $50 for both of us there and back, but we cannot go by local car."

"Why?"

"Because journalists can only go by private car, and sometimes they take a guard with the Kalashnikov."

"But that's not necessary now. Is it? Isn't it safe to go to Kabul now?"

"Yes, it's safe, but we will not get permission to go by local car."

"Then we won't ask for permission; we'll just go."

"But this will be very bad for me." He says this in the most forlorn way, as a sad sigh, as if I am asking him to cut off one of his fingers.

"Then I'll go alone, and that way you won't get in any trouble."

"But I must go with you," he says. "I promised you I would not leave your side, and so I can only go where you go. If you want, we can ask to go by local car. Maybe they will say yes."

"But it's late now and the ministry is closed and I'd like to leave tomorrow morning."

"We can ask the man here in the hotel."

"Which man?"

"The man in the office."

"I thought he was the manager of the hotel."

"He works for the ministry of foreign affairs."

"But he's always here."

"Yes, because all foreigners are staying here."

"Then why do you always go across the street to the office to ask permission any time we go somewhere?"

"Because there is another man, a bigger man," he says in a way that I know means the conversation is over.

We go downstairs, where the man from foreign affairs is in his office, sitting next to the woodstove. Najibullah tells him our plans, and he asks us to sit down.

"We are asking that all journalists travel to Kabul in private cars with armed guards," he says, "because we can't be certain of your safety. It's a long way, and out of our district."

I think this is just a way to squeeze more money out of me, but I don't say this. "It's very important for my story," I say, "that I travel in a local car."

"Aren't you afraid?" he asks.

"No, I'm not," I say. "Everyone I've met here has been very friendly and helpful. I haven't had any trouble with anyone, and this is what I would like to write for my magazine, which is read by millions of Americans. I would like to tell them that Afghanistan is a good place and that they should come here on vacation, but how can I say this if I travel with an armed guard? I need to take a local car and travel with other Afghans."

"But we can't be sure of your safety."

"No, but then, who can? My fate is in God's hands, is it not?"

"Yes, certainly. Inshallah."

I had him. "Inshallah, then, so it's okay?"

"Yes, we will try it this once," he says, "but please if you would send word back with the driver, saying that you have made it safely so we do not worry."

We leave the hotel just before dawn and take a taxi to the place where the local cars meet. Najibullah tells me to stay in the car while he goes in to buy two tickets. If they see me, he says, they will charge much more for my ticket. He comes back and says, "Okay, let's go. Follow me." I get out and all the men who are standing around start yelling at once: "*Horiji!*" "*Horiji!*" (Foreign Devil! Foreign Devil!).

"Quickly," Najibullah says, "please, get inside the car."

"What are they saying?"

"Never mind. Just get in the car."

"Tell me what they are saying so I can respond," I say. Najibullah looks at me with a blank stare for a second and then turns and yells at the crowd, and they back off and quiet down. We get in the car and he tells me the men were saying that I am a rich man and it's not fair that I buy a regular ticket, so they wanted to take something from me. He told them I am a very famous writer and that if they didn't stop bothering me I would tell all Americans that Afghanistan is full of bad men and that nobody should ever come here. It worked. Now we have a man with a machine gun standing by the front of the car, on guard, although he is allowing a little kid to press his face up against my window and stare, only inches away.

The car is a Toyota Corolla sedan. Three other passengers get in, so with the driver that's six. Najibullah sits in the middle up front, shifting the gears for the driver between his legs. We drive east out of the city across the flat desert, skirting the foothills of the Hindu Kush. I crack my window because it's steaming up. I look for the mountains, but it's a grey and foggy morning and I can't see a thing except sand dunes. It could be the Atacama.

After fifty miles it's getting light and the fog has lifted and I can see the base of the mountain wall, impenetrable except for a narrow slit, a vagina-like entrance. We turn and head straight for it. The canyon is only fifty feet wide at the bottom, room enough for only a river and a road between vertical cliffs of volcanic rock. The driver points out the rusted carcass of a Russian helicopter smashed into the cliffs three hundred feet overhead.

There are bomb craters in the road—twelve feet wide and six feet deep—and the burned-out shells of Toyota pickups off to the side. The Taliban came through here when they fled Mazar and U.S. planes took out some of them. The driver has to slow down and weave between wreckage, and he starts complaining. He says this was a good road before the Americans bombed it. He wants to know if somebody is going to come and fill in the holes.

"Yes, for sure," I say. "We have special machines for doing this, they're called bulldozers, very big and strong, and we have so many that we don't know what to do with them." In my notebook, I jot a reminder to call the road department upon my return.

The narrow canyon opens onto a wide, flat valley. It's circular, thirty to forty miles in diameter, surrounded by mountains, and in the center of the circle is a volcanic plug—the valley is a caldera. The surrounding mountains are sunbaked dirt, like the skin of an elephant. They're either heavily overgrazed or they've never, ever, had anything growing on them.

"Is it okay if I smoke?" I ask. I'm hungry and because it's Ramadan there's little chance we'll be stopping to eat.

"Yes, go ahead," the driver says.

"But is smoking against the rules of Ramadan?"

"Yes, everything is against the rules of Ramadan," he says. "It is forbidden even to smell a flower, or to look at a beautiful young girl. We can have no pleasures during the day, but at night anything is possible."

"But it's okay if I break the rules?"

"For you it is not breaking the rules. You are a Christian and have your own book, and so for you it is not forbidden, am I right?"

"You're right. In fact, Jesus smoked hashish."

"No, I think this is not true," he says.

"Well, maybe not," I say, "but Mohammed smoked hashish, didn't he?"

"No, sir," he says, "I am telling you that this is not true. Where did you hear this?"

"From a Russian," I say. I'm making all this up and realize I'm bordering on rudeness, but I want to see how he'll react. I grew up with religious fanatics, among the Mormons, and sometimes I can't help myself.

"The Russians do not believe in God," he says. "You must not listen to what they tell you." Everybody in the car seems to agree on this.

"Well," I say, "what about the deal with women? I haven't seen one woman since I've been here who hasn't been under a burkha. Don't you wish you could look at women, you know, just look at them?"

The driver is stunned. A *horiji* speaking of wanting to see Afghan women is too much of an affront. So Najibullah takes over, trying to smooth things out by telling me that perhaps with the Taliban gone the women will someday take off their burkhas, perhaps at the university, but that it's not such a good thing because these women might be beaten by their husbands or fathers.

"That's how it used to be," I say, "but don't you think it will change?"

"No," he says, "it will not change because it's what we

believe. The Taliban believed this, but we also believe it, the Pashtun people."

"So have you ever gone on a date?" I ask him.

"What's a date?" he says.

"Like when you go somewhere with a girl and maybe hold her hand or kiss her."

"No, I've never done this," he says. "I've never even spoken with a girl other than my sisters. If I speak with a girl in this way then our fathers would beat us with a stick."

"What if you actually had sex with a girl?"

"Then we would both be beaten many more times and forced to marry each other."

"What if when you are married, or not you, but someone else is married and his wife has sex with another man?"

"Then she will be killed with the Kalashnikov," he says as a matter of fact.

"Who would kill her?"

"Her father or her brother."

"I don't believe that."

"It's true, believe me."

"You would do this? To your own sister?"

"Yes, I would have to, for my family."

"No," I say, putting my hand on his shoulder, "Najib, I know you and you wouldn't kill your own sister. I'm sorry, I wasn't really serious before, but this is a serious thing. You wouldn't kill your sister."

"Yes, I would!" he says, angrily. "First, it is my father's responsibility. If he doesn't do it, then my biggest brother must do it. If not he, then my next smaller brother, and then my next brother, to me, and I'm telling you serious I would do it."

To drive home the point he tells the other men what he's saying and they all nod their heads—yes, she must be killed.

"With a Kalashnikov?" I ask.

"Or by putting the stones on top of her," the driver adds, all of them looking at me with stern faces.

I give up.

"Yes, of course," I say. "Luckily, you guys got plenty of stones around here." I make another note, a prescription for Afghanistan—bulldozers and LSD.

From the plain of the caldera the road goes into a broad canyon with pastures and irrigated fields. The mountains are in front of us, hidden behind the clouds. The ascent is gradual, with a lot of switchbacks and avalanche sheds, all constructed by the Soviets and marked every mile or so by one of their tanks, left to rust as monuments. At eight thousand feet there's snow and ice on the road and our driver gets out and ties on some chains with rope. At nine thousand feet it's snowing.

I can't see very far because of the clouds, but the slope we're traversing is very steep. Maybe I'd ski it if it was sunny and I could see what's above and below, but today it would be like jumping into a cloud. I feel much better when we're under the avalanche sheds and not exposed to I don't know how many thousands of feet of hanging snowfields. Luckily, there are a lot of sheds, covered with a concrete roof but open to the downward slope so you can see out down the valley, or could, if it wasn't a whiteout.

The road ends at the Salang Tunnel, elevation 11,154 feet above sea level, just under the elevation of the Eisenhower tunnel through the Rockies in Colorado. This tunnel, built by the Soviets in 1964, cuts travel time from Mazar to Kabul from three days to ten hours. The roads ends here, at least for cars and trucks, because the tunnel was blown up, twice, in the mid-1990s by the Tajik commander Ahmed Shah Massoud, "the Lion of Panjshir," who was killed a few days before September 11 by suspected Al Qaeda agents posing as television reporters. Massoud cut off the tunnel as a military tactic to keep the Taliban from moving north, and it worked for a little while, until the Taliban came north on the old road, which has many ups and downs, over passes, through steep valleys. The old road goes through Bamiyan, where the Taliban destroyed the stone Buddhas.

We get out of the car and start to walk through a blizzard. The actual entrance to the tunnel is still a kilometer away, mainly through avalanche sheds. There are a lot of men and boys at the place where you start walking. They're porters, standing in the snow with bare ankles and plastic slippers. They want to carry my pack and I tell them no. They get upset and grab at it and I push their arms away and tell them to back off. They're acting like it's a union deal and I don't have a choice in the matter, but it's just not going to happen that way. My pack stays on my back.

"Come quickly," Najibullah says, "and you must walk exactly where I step. There are still land mines here." I think he's exaggerating the risk and maybe freaking out a bit from the high alpine conditions—the blizzard, the thin air. Or maybe it's that I don't want to consider land mines to be a real possibility due to my lifelong fear of losing a limb. I flash back to the foot at Qala-i-Jhangi, the opposite of a land mine, where the body was gone but the foot was intact. I'm not going to think about it.

The north entrance to the tunnel is clear and we can walk right in, but once inside there's rebar and slabs of concrete and sections of ventilation ducts lying everywhere on the ground, and we have to turn on our headlamps and move carefully so as to not get jabbed or tripped. Then it gets worse. We're climbing over and ducking under fallen supports, big slabs of concrete hanging down from the ceiling. There are many other people inside—women with little kids crying, porters with huge boxes on their backs held with a tumpline around their foreheads, workers salvaging scraps of metal and huddling around small fires to stay warm—and the air is so full of smoke that every flashlight makes a distinct cone that fades into darkness.

All the goods and materials moving between the north and south of Afghanistan are carried on the backs of porters through this hellish passageway. It's the perfect example of why fighting a war in these mountains is so difficult. By cutting off this road, you cut off travel not only from Kabul but from Rawalpindi and Delhi in the south to Dushanbe and Tashkent and Ashgabat in the north. In these mountains, with a few well-placed bombs, you can paralyze a large part of the Asian subcontinent.

The tunnel is two kilometers long and it takes an hour to get through moving as fast as we can go without running. The south portal has been blown apart, so we have to go up and over a tall, icy mound of debris, and then we're out.

It's still snowing, although there's no wind on this side. Just beyond the portal are more taxis and trucks, another crowd of men. I walk up and they all start yelling, a barrage of accusations and threats. I don't know the specifics because Najib has vanished. I look for guns and don't see any, but they try to surround me; they try to stand in front of me. I keep walking. I'm not worried about a fight—I'm bigger than they are, and they're wearing plastic slippers in the snow. So I try to act like a British officer from back in the colonial days—"Let's have some fair play here, men, for the good of the Queen, carry on." Najibullah reappears; he's found a car, tells me to get in.

"What were they saying?" I ask.

"When you came out of the tunnel, they were saying you are a foreigner and you are alone and they should take your money and kill you."

"But they didn't have any guns."

"Yes, they have guns. And knives, like this," he says, pulling out a four-inch stiletto. "They hide them."

"Najib," I say, "put that away. Act like we're supposed to be here, like we're doing our job, and they won't mess with us."

"If you had a job, then you would have bodyguards, and they know this," he says, sort of freaking out.

"All they know is I'm not afraid of them," I say, "and right now they're wondering why. By the time they come up with a plan, we'll be gone."

Again there are six of us in a Toyota Corolla. The driver speeds down the mountain, hurrying to get to Kabul before dark. Three times we cross the river in the bottom of the canyon, and at each crossing there's a concrete bridge that was blown up by Massoud's troops. In place of the larger concrete bridges they've made smaller bridges down close to the water by piling up big mounds of dirt, sometimes using Russian tanks for buttresses, and spanning the distance with metal planks from dismembered tank frames. Nothing larger than a small truck can pass over these bridges, and none faster than a breathless crawl.

We arrive at the outskirts of Kabul at dusk. The city sits in a huge crater under a cloud of dust. The road is lined with shipping containers filled with scraps of metal, car wheels, motorcycle frames, doors, and firewood. In front of the containers there are men standing around, pounding metal, sawing wood, fixing horse carts, and cutting up empty cans. Our driver is swimming through traffic—honking, stopping, going. I ask Najibullah a question at the same time the guy on the other side of the backseat says something to him. I say, "Do these people live in those containers?" but Najibullah chooses to translate for the other guy. "This man thinks you have a very beautiful face and he would like to give his love to you." No one is laughing but me, so I stop and let the comment fade with the light.

We stay with Najibullah's uncle and his family. They live in a blighted proletarian housing complex, the exterior walls pocked by bullet holes, the stairways fetid with decaying waste, electrical wires rupturing out of circuit boxes like burnt snakes. No running water. But in Kabul this is a good place, a middle-class place.

I wait in the stairway while Najibullah goes in to say hello and make sure his aunt is in another room before I come in. His uncle is a very gracious man, thirty-five years old, who tells me, in English, that he's honored to have an American guest in his home. We sit in the guest room on mattresses resting on Afghan carpets.

"Would you like some tea and bread?" he asks, carefully separating each word and rolling the *r* in bread. "In Afghanistan we give our guests everything. While you are in my house, whatever you need, you have."

He's beaming at me as if I am a rare jewel, and three of his little children are climbing over each other holding themselves back from petting me like a new puppy.

I've read that Afghans consider themselves to be the ultimate hosts. For instance, once a man is invited into an Afghan home, his hosts will die trying to protect him from his enemies, but at the same time they won't let him meet or even look at their women.

"What was it like when the United States was bombing the city?" I ask. "Did bombs fall close to here?"

"Yes," he says, "every night, some only five or six blocks from here. Big bombs, very big bombs. I could not sleep; my children were very afraid."

"Did the bombs kill civilians or did they hit military targets?"

"They hit the military targets, but some civilians were died."

"How many?"

"I think one hundred or one hundred and fifty."

"And is that a lot or not that many?"

"I think it is not that many. We are very happy the Taliban are finished. I am engineer, but I have no work for four years. I work only some days as chauffeur. I want very much to work for my family."

"What do you think America should do to help?"

"America should give peacekeeping force here to take guns. There are many, many guns, and there are many fighting for Afghan people. If America or United Nations peacekeeping force do not come here then it will be very bad, worse than before the Taliban. But they will come, it is true?"

"I don't know," I say. "Maybe, maybe not." I don't want to lie to him.

The next morning another uncle of Najibullah's drives us around the city in his taxicab. We go by the lamppost where the Taliban hung the body of President Najibullah. We drive by the soccer stadium where the Taliban conducted public executions. Then we go to the zoo, which has been bombarded by mortar shells. There are a lot of empty cages with big holes in the walls, but there are still some animals alive—some monkeys, some hawks and eagles and vultures, and a lion that looks senile and is missing an eye due to a grenade thrown by a man seeking revenge after his brother went in the cage and the lion ate him. In an open area between the animal houses there's a shipping container riddled with bullets and blown up from the inside out—its walls approaching spherical—sitting by itself as a piece of sculpture. Conceptual art.

Beyond the container is the Kabul River, which after three years of drought is not much more than a series of festering pools. Still, there are people using the water—bathing in it, drinking it, and filling buckets to wash taxicabs.

Just outside the gates of the zoo there's an entire neighborhood demolished by bombardments—acres and acres of adobe buildings in ruins. I'm starting to see everything as conceptual art.

"What happened here?" I ask Najibullah.

"It was the Hazara people who were living here, and Massoud's army shelled them from that hill."

"Why?"

"Because they are Hazara people and Massoud's people are Tajik," he says, as if I should know this already, as if it were a natural phenomenon like the sun coming up in the morning.

"This was before the Taliban took over?"

"Yes, when the Taliban came they stopped this fighting."

This is why, in the years and months preceding 9/11, the United States actually supported the Taliban as an ally—they were the only force capable of stopping the various ethnic factions in Afghanistan from killing each other. Compared with this kind of devastation, it was expedient to overlook the public executions of women in the soccer stadium, the imposition of sharia, and the harboring of Osama bin Laden.

"What a fucking mess," I say. "I'm sorry."

"How long would it take in America to rebuild this place?" Najibullah asks.

"Oh, shit," I say, "in America it might take three years."

"And then it will be as good as Tashkent?"

"Well," I say, "anyplace in America is better than Tashkent, even if it's strip malls and parking lots. But it's not going to happen like that; at least, I hope it doesn't happen like that. Maybe America will give Afghanistan some money for rebuilding, but the work, how the city is rebuilt, should be done by the Afghan people."

"And how long will that take?"

"I don't know, maybe fifty years, maybe longer if everybody keeps hating each other for being from a different tribe."

"But I will be an old man by then."

"Yes," I say, "you would be. My advice is you should find a way to get out of here."

"Where will I go?"

"Anywhere. The world is a big place and there are a lot of things to see. A lot of opportunities."

"But I think this is not possible for me."

I don't know what to tell him. If his family had any money, they would have left years ago, along with the rest of the middle class, during the Soviet occupation. Most of the people who stayed are poor and have no modern skills. It will take a long time, maybe forever, to make this place look even as good as Tashkent, and then it will still suck.

Najibullah just looks at the ground and kicks a brick and says, "Shit."

The One Mighty and Strong
Salt Lake City, 2002–2010

Temple Square attracts religious wackos like moths to a flame. They stand outside the wall yelling condemnations, calling for repentance, quoting from the Bible. Or they pose quietly in costumes, such as the young man with his face painted silver, dressed as Little Bo Peep. Or Worm, who sat naked below the Brigham Young statue with the letters W-O-R-M tattooed across his forehead. Or Brian David Mitchell, the man who dressed like Jesus Christ and stole fourteen-year-old Elizabeth Smart from her bed in the middle of the night. We knew him as a temple moth and thought he was crazy but harmless. This is why we didn't suspect him, even when he walked around downtown with Elizabeth in tow, her face covered by a veil. It's about the strangest thing that's ever happened in Salt Lake City, and it could only have happened here, in this place and time, perhaps caused by the aura emanating from the Temple itself.

Hearken! Oh ye inhabitants of the earth. Listen together and open your ears, for it is I, the Lord God of all the Earth, the creator of all things that speaketh unto you.

So opens the twenty-seven-page prophecy of Immanuel David Isaiah, the name Mitchell adopted once he realized he was the messenger of God, the new prophet on Earth.

I have raised up my servant Immanuel David Isaiah, ever my righteous right hand, to be a light and a covenant to my people—to all those who will repent and come unto me, for in my servant, Immanuel is the fullness of my gospel.

In the prophecy, God proclaims Immanuel to be "the one mighty and strong" called to set His house in order before the Apocalypse, a task requiring the aid of seven times seven virgin wives, plus one. His legal wife at the time, Wanda Barzee, carefully transcribed the prophecy in longhand and made copies to circulate among family and friends.

Then they abducted their first virgin, Elizabeth Smart, and took her, on foot, up into the hills above her home in Federal Heights, where they had a camp in some scrub oak. There, that first night, Mitchell performed a sacred wedding ceremony, and then he raped her.

She was abducted June 5, 2002, and she was gone for nine months.

It happened in my neighborhood, so I remember it. I didn't know her, but my son went to grade school with her and we had a photo of the two of them together at a birthday party—she was a princess and he was a cowboy. She was taken from her bedroom in the middle of the night, and everyone was terrorized. If this could happen to the Smart family, then no one was safe. Their multimillion-dollar home represented the core values of Mormon traditions. Their extended family reached back to the original pioneers and into the present-day church hierarchy. It was like 9/11, only the news spread by telephone instead of TV—women calling women and the men saying "What? What happened?"

A man took Elizabeth from her bed.

It was the beginning of summer and unusually hot, the air above the valley standing still, loud crickets in the backyard that would not shut up. A valley of hearts cracked open.

Thousands of volunteers combed the neighborhood, looking in window wells, going through stacks of wood. They covered the foothills in broad lines, calling her name. I didn't volunteer because I didn't think I could handle that part, hearing her name called out.

The police arrested a suspect, Richard Ricci, but the poor man died while in custody from a ruptured artery in his brain. He didn't take Elizabeth; no one but the police thought he was the guy.

Throughout the summer, Elizabeth's photo hung in every window of every shop and on every lamppost. Her father and her family appeared regularly on local, national, and international news programs, begging and weeping for her safe return. It seemed she was hidden somewhere far away, somewhere just beyond the broadcasting spectrum, like the scene in *The Wizard of Oz* in which Dorothy's family calls to her through the crystal ball.

Then, when she was found nine months later, in March 2003, we realized she'd actually been right here in front of us, walking around downtown, reading in the library, eating in fast-food restaurants, and going to parties with Mitchell and his wife, Wanda Barzee. From June until August they hid out in their camp in the scrub oak up in the foothills, avoiding the search parties. Then they began coming down into the city by day, passing within a quarter-mile of Elizabeth's home. They walked the streets dressed as religious pilgrims from the New Testament. Mitchell had a long beard and a walking stick. Elizabeth and Wanda covered everything but their eyes. And no one figured it out.

In late October they got on a bus and went to San Diego, where they spent the winter, also camping out. In March 2003, they came back to Salt Lake, and Elizabeth was discovered walking down State Street wearing a grey wig and sunglasses. The first thing she said to the police was, "I know who you think I am. You guys think I'm that Elizabeth Smart girl who ran away."

Mitchell was arrested, and the state courts tried to determine whether he was competent to stand trial. In the fall of 2008, after six years, the federal courts stepped in, ordering new psychological evaluations. This whole delay was very annoying. It seemed crazy we couldn't determine whether Mitchell was crazy, and there were other questions, important questions, no one was talking about, such as, "Why didn't she run away or cry out for help?" And, "Why didn't we recognize her—how was she able to stand right in front of us and become invisible?"

You'd think it wouldn't be so hard to answer these questions, but for us it's like groping about in a dark room—we know the answers are here somewhere, but we just can't find them. Or, actually, it's that we don't even want to ask the questions because we know the answers don't make sense, at least not to the rational mind or in a court of law. They only make sense in and around the Temple. To understand how this works we need to go back in time, back to the beginning of the Mormon Church.

When Joseph Smith was a boy, circa 1820, his family moved from New Hampshire to the "burnt over district" of western New York. The area earned this name because it was so full of Christian evangelists preaching revivalism as to have no fuel (people) left to burn (convert). Joseph, age fourteen, went to the woods, knelt down, and began to pray to God, asking Him which religion is true. God appeared to Joseph as a light brighter than sun and told him that all religions had become corrupted, and that he, Joseph, had been chosen to be the new prophet and restore the true gospel. Ten years later, in 1830, Joseph published the Book of Mormon, establishing a new church and a new people, the Latter-Day Saints, or Mormons.

In the early days of the Church, Joseph Smith taught his followers that there was only a thin veil separating this temporal plane from the celestial realm, and that by praying in the proper manner and performing certain rituals they could part the veil and have magical and mystical experiences with angels and gods and demons who had human bodies filled with white spirit fluid instead of blood. Yes, according to Joseph Smith, there was and is more than one god and more than one devil. He said we have only one Heavenly Father and he is a god, but there are many other gods with their own planets in other places in the universe. Joseph told his followers, in essence, "There are gods and angels among us and I have contacted them; they are my friends. You can know them too, if you only follow my instructions."

Lots of people at the time—living on the frontier, surrounded by stumps and mud, so alone on the big continent—thought it was a good idea. Joseph's followers began speaking in tongues and healing the sick and having visions and revelations. They pitied members of other faiths who did not have these experiences, and thought this alone was proof Joseph Smith had indeed restored the gospel on Earth.

Everything went fine until Smith's right-hand man, his "assistant president," Oliver Cowdery, began speaking directly to God, our Heavenly Father, and God told him that Joseph Smith had become corrupt and now he, Oliver Cowdery, was the new prophet who held the keys to the kingdom of heaven. Joseph responded by saying Cowdery had not been speaking to God but to Satan, and he excommunicated him.

After that, Joseph prophesied that a member of the church can only receive personal revelation concerning matters within his own "stewardship," his own domain of authority and control. Therefore, if a man has a wife and children, he may receive revelation from God concerning decisions he must make about his wife and children, and they must obey him, just as he must, in turn, obey those men in higher positions of the church hierarchy, all the way up to the Prophet, who has stewardship over every member of the church.

In this way, obedience to authority became the flip side of prophecy, visions, and speaking in tongues. This is the razor's edge of Mormonism. You are supposed to seek the truth by having direct mystical experiences with spirits and supernatural forces, while at the same time blindly following orders coming down through a social bureaucracy. Many, especially in the early days, didn't like these lines of authority and control and chose to contact the spirit world directly. In 1909, the tenth president of the church, Joseph Fielding Smith, wrote:

> There never was a time, perhaps, when there were more false prophets than there are today . . . We get letters from them, and commands and threats from them, and admonitions and warnings and revelations from them, nearly every day . . . some calling themselves "deliverers of Israel," some calling themselves "the one mighty and strong, who is to deliver Israel out of bondage." . . . We have these letters—those that we have not destroyed—stacked up almost by the cord. Some of these false prophets, these men to "deliver Israel," and these foolish, unwise, unstable creatures, led about by every wind of doctrine have risen right in our own midst.
>
> (*LDS Conference Report*, October 1909, p. 9)

In the modern Mormon Church, contact with the spirit world is managed through rituals enacted in the Temple. Inside, there are rooms depicting the world before and after the Fall of Man. Then there is the Celestial Room, which depicts the highest realm of heaven. Inside the Celestial Room, there's a smaller room called the Holy of Holies, and when the Prophet of the Church wants to talk to God, he goes inside the Holy of Holies. There he receives revelation concerning Church doctrine and affairs. Everyone else stays in the Celestial Room and performs the sacred ritual of being "pulled through the veil."

There's an actual veil there, and live actors portraying God, resurrected beings, and the apostles Peter, James, and John. They reach through the veil and pull patrons across to the other side, the Celestial Kingdom. This is a very sacred and very real thing for Mormons, like a trip to heaven and back. However, in order to get into the temple you have to have a recommendation from your bishop, and to get a recommendation you have to be a member in "good standing," and to be in good standing you must follow a lot of rules. Most Mormons try to follow the rules, and most can get a temple recommendation if they want.

Mormons still believe in personal revelation, but Church authorities now tend to downplay direct communication with God and instead encourage communion with the Holy Ghost, a warm and fuzzy experience sometimes described as a "burning in the bosom." In order to survive and grow, the Mormon Church has become progressively more mainstream and status quo; for instance, the Mormons now allow black men to hold the priesthood and no longer practice "blood atonement" rituals in the temple. In 1996, President and Prophet Gordon B. Hinckley told Mike Wallace on *60 Minutes*, "We're reaching out across the world. We're not a weird people."

Still, sometimes there are "weird" ones among them, such as Brian David Mitchell's father, Shirl Mitchell, who not only received word from God that he was the Christ, but then transcribed visions and revelations revealing an entirely new cosmology, which he combined into a nine-hundred-page manuscript titled "Spokesman for the Infant God or Goddess."

According to Mormon historian John-Charles Duffy (perhaps the only person who's ever read the manuscript),

> Shirl teaches that human beings collectively constitute the body of an infant deity, just as cells constitute our own bodies. The infant deity—the offspring of the sun, who is a goddess, and a male companion star—has been gestating over the last several million years of human evolution and is now ready to be born. This birth will occasion a radical transformation in society. In the new age following the birth of the infant deity, people will follow an all-natural vegetarian diet. Children will engage in erotic play without repression; teenagers will freely copulate for the purpose of procreation; and adults, having sexually satiated themselves during childhood and adolescence, will live in celibate ecstasy. . . . Shirl writes of the "addictive voyeurism" that had him fondling young girls as a child and peeping into women's windows as an adult. He complains that every woman is a manipulative nymphomaniac whom no husband could possible satisfy; he fears that his penis could be "strangled" during sex; he is fascinated by a recurring dream in which a shaft of light penetrates his anal chakra. Accused by his former wife of rape, Shirl defends himself by insisting that when rape occurs in marriage, it's because wives withhold sex from their husbands and that there can be no "illegal rape" in a marriage anyway.
>
> (John Charles Duffy, "The Making of Immanuel," *Sunstone*, October 2003, p. 36)

Shirl and his wife had six children, and Brian David was the third, born in 1953. They lived in a middle-class suburban neighborhood at the base of the Wasatch Mountains. As a child, Brian was a Cub Scout and played sports and went to church on Sundays, but when he was sixteen, according to his father, Brian was found guilty of exposing himself to a child and sent to a juvenile delinquent hall. At nineteen, he impregnated a sixteen-year-old girl and then married her. They had two children and then got divorced. He married again, to a woman who had three kids already, and together they had two more. Then they got divorced. Then his ex-wife, Debbie Mitchell, accused him of molesting their children. Then he married a woman eight years his senior, Wanda Barzee, who already had six children.

Until he was nearly thirty years old, Mitchell moved in and out of the church, sometimes professing to be an atheist. Then, according to Derrick Thompson, Mitchell's stepson, he ate a large dose of LSD out in the Utah desert and realized God wanted him back in the Mormon Church. So, with his third wife, Wanda Barzee, he set out to become a member in good standing. He worked as a die cutter in a jewelry store; she studied the organ, hoping to someday play in the Tabernacle. He became the second counselor to the bishop, a member of the church hierarchy, and volunteered to work in the temple as a live actor.

In the Salt Lake Temple there's a ritual known as "the endowment" in which volunteer actors portray characters from the Old Testament and dramatize the story of man's fall from grace in the Garden of Eden. Mitchell played Satan, a part that required him to loudly proclaim that he is the incarnation of evil and has bought up armies and popes to work his will upon mankind. Mitchell loved this part and even bragged that his temple coworkers had told him, "You're one of the best we've ever had, but can you tone it down a little bit?"

After this, Mitchell and Barzee quit their regular jobs in Salt Lake and hit the road, hitchhiking around the country for two years as itinerant preachers. When they returned in 1997 they were dressed as religious pilgrims and insisting their friends and family call them by their new names— Immanuel David Isaiah and God Adorneth.

Mitchell became a well-known beggar and pest around the downtown area, standing outside the shopping mall across the street from Temple Square, sometimes cursing people if they didn't give him money, or spreading his arms, portraying Jesus suffering on the cross. In April 2002, he finished his twenty-seven-page revelation titled "The Book of Immanuel David Isaiah" and gave copies to friends and relatives. Somehow Church authorities obtained a copy, and at the beginning of June 2002, the same week he took Elizabeth Smart, Brian David Mitchell was excommunicated.

This may sound like a strange story to people who are not from around here, but everything that happened in Mitchell's life, at least to the point at which he kidnapped Elizabeth, is not that unusual within the Mormon community. Most Mormons do not have visitations and revelations, but some still do, and when it happens there tend to be dramatic consequences.

For example, in 1993, while LDS Apostle Howard Hunter was addressing fifteen thousand BYU students in their basketball arena, a young man named Cody Judy appeared on stage and stood behind Hunter with a briefcase he said contained a bomb. He gave Hunter a three-page letter describing how God had made him, Cody Judy, the new prophet of the church, and told Hunter to read it or he would blow everybody up. There was no bomb in the briefcase, only a Book of Mormon. Judy was taken to the state mental hospital. But then he escaped by jumping out of his third-story window and running into the mountains. For three weeks he traveled "like a deer," fearing a massive manhunt. Then, suddenly, he showed up at the Church-owned television station and asked for some airtime on the news. Then he spent eight years in prison, and when he got out he worked in a video store and ran for public office. Now he has a Facebook site.

I had a friend in high school who was a gifted athlete and a charming young man. His family lived down the street from mine, next to the Salt Lake Country Club. Late one summer night, he burst into my bedroom, very frightened. He said he'd been making out with his girlfriend on the ninth green and his guardian angel appeared in a glowing light above a sand trap. The angel told him to take his hand out of his girlfriend's pants and not to put it back, ever again.

At the time, no one mentioned schizophrenia. We all thought it was just part of being a Mormon—even when he attacked his father because he thought he was the Devil, even when he would go down to Temple Square and walk up to young women and tell them that God had just told him they were to be married in the Celestial Kingdom. We thought this was strange, but not necessarily out of the ordinary.

His family sent him on a mission, thinking it would be good for him, but it only made him more crazy. He came back and went into the psych ward at the university hospital, where they put him on heavy medication. He struggled through a marriage and numerous low-paying jobs and volunteered as a live actor in the Temple, portraying "Heavenly Father Behind the Veil," but his health went downhill fast and he died at age twenty-nine due to organ failure from all the medication he was taking. I still miss that guy. He once laid his hands upon my head and gave me a blessing.

Then there was the group of polygamists in central Utah who claimed to be receiving "unanimous revelations," where not one but all ten men would receive the same revelation at the same time. Angels and apostles and resurrected beings had appeared to them, and they had seen and heard many wonderful things. For instance, they were told by unanimous revelation that they were all new prophets and they should start a new church called the "True and Living Church of Jesus Christ of the Last Days," which they did. Then God told them that they should become polygamists, which they did. Then, unfortunately, God told only some of them that they should sleep with more than one wife in the bed at a time, which they did, and this caused their quorum of ten apostles to break apart, as some considered the practice to be an abomination unto the Lord.

Prophecy and polygamy often go together. When God speaks to a man and tells him he is the new prophet and must now take charge of the only true church, the next thing He often tells the man is to become a polygamist. Part of the responsibility of being the new prophet is to spread "the seed of David" and produce the new chosen people. This takes a lot of women and a lot of effort.

Many people in Salt Lake City, Mormon and non-Mormon, are opposed to polygamy, but very few are in favor of prosecuting and punishing the crime. There are a lot of polygamists in these parts, and it would be very expensive and socially chaotic to go after them. Polygamy is a long-established part of the local culture, and, in addition, we all live in something that resembles a polygamous culture, where affairs and serial monogamy are common. So who will be the first to throw a stone? And what would come from it?

In this way we tolerate polygamy, apparently even among crazy homeless people dressed as characters from the New Testament. People who saw Mitchell walking around downtown with Wanda and Elizabeth in tow assumed he had taken a young polygamist wife, and nobody questioned him about it, even though the new wife looked very young.

All that separated her from us was the veil she wore over her nose and mouth. If she had taken off the veil, we would have recognized her. We thought she had either been killed or was being held against her will by someone who was a monster. No one imagined she would be walking around with a man who thought he was Jesus Christ.

Although her father now denies it, Elizabeth may have been suffering from the Stockholm syndrome, also known as terror or trauma bonding, in which victims display compassion for and even loyalty to their captors. It's common in cases of abused children, battered women, prisoners of war, cult members, incest victims, and concentration camp prisoners. The victim feels intense fear of physical harm. All control is in the hands of the captor. If the captor then shows the victim some kindness, the victim often begins to support and sympathize with the abuser's reasons and behaviors, even at times helping him and not trying to escape. In the late 1970s, Patty Hearst was kidnapped by the Symbionese

Liberation Army, and then helped them rob a bank. Jaycee Lee Dugard was kidnapped in 1991 when she was eleven years old by Phillip Craig Garrido, with whom she eventually had two daughters. When she was found in 2009, she told the authorities that Garrido was a "great person" who was "good with her kids."

Stockholm syndrome seems like a good explanation for why Elizabeth didn't cry out or run away, and perhaps Elizabeth's father, Ed Smart, now denies this explanation because he is unwilling to accept that Elizabeth ever supported or sympathized with Mitchell, let alone that she believed he was the new prophet. Elizabeth has testified in Federal Court that she saw Mitchell as "evil, wicked, manipulative, sneaky, slimy, selfish, greedy, not spiritual, not religious, and not close to God." She said Mitchell threatened to kill her and her family if she ran away. But, really, there were many opportunities, in public, when all she had to do was take off the veil . . . unless she believed Mitchell actually had magical powers. And maybe he did.

In late August, the threesome went to a party thrown by a gang of bohemians just down the hill from Elizabeth's home. It can get quite hot here in August during the day, but the nights are enjoyable. I imagine Mitchell and Barzee and Elizabeth had been walking around town all day in the heat and were on their way back up to the foothills on a cool evening, and they passed by a house with a party going on, so they crashed it. Mitchell liked to drink beer, and free beer was hard to pass up. The house had a nickname, China Blue, and a reputation for wild parties with people often coming in costume, so the pilgrim robes and polygamy theme didn't seem that out of place.

The host of the party, a man named Bub, told me he was a little perplexed that this guy who was spouting religious doctrine was also pounding down a lot of beer. He said somebody pulled out some homemade absinthe, and Mitchell tried to get Elizabeth to drink some, but she refused.

A couple of young women at the party started talking to Elizabeth. The women could only see her eyes, but they thought she looked uncomfortable and asked her if she was okay, if she needed any help. She wouldn't talk to them. Mitchell then came up and pulled her by the arm into another room. This upset Bub and his friends, and they confronted Mitchell on his harsh treatment of the young woman. Under attack, Mitchell jumped up on a chair and started hurling fire and brimstone at the guests, invoking scripture and the power of the Lord and damning them all to hell—perhaps in the voice he perfected while portraying Satan in the Temple. He was still yelling as they pushed him out the door. Then he stood in the front yard and yelled some more before taking his women and going home, back to their camp high in the foothills. But Mitchell was so intoxicated he only made it as far as the university golf course, where he passed out on the grass, Wanda and Elizabeth going on without him.

Bub told me he felt kind of dumb when he realized the girl he was trying to protect was Elizabeth Smart, thereby missing the $250,000 reward. He said, "It was very mysterious, the whole scenario, almost like he was using black magic to build a psychic fence around the situation."

The legal definition of insanity rests upon the question of whether the accused knew he was doing something wrong. I think we should apply this test to Mitchell on that August night as he stood in the yard on Second South and condemned the partiers at China Blue. Imagine, here is a man who has abducted and raped a young girl, and she has a $250,000 reward on her head, and he is raving, late at night, condemning people to hell in a front yard less than a mile from her home.

Did he know this was wrong?

I think he thought he was the prophet, acting in God's name. I think he thought it was right, if not absolutely necessary. So he was insane, for sure.

But then what about the time, shortly after the party on Second South, when Mitchell, Barzee, and Elizabeth were confronted by a homicide detective in the library downtown? The detective had been told of a report that Elizabeth Smart was in disguise at the library. He approached the three and asked Elizabeth to take off her veil, but Mitchell stepped in and somehow Jedi mind-tricked the officer into backing off and leaving them alone by telling him Elizabeth was his daughter and it was against their religion for her to show her face or speak in public. The officer said Mitchell stayed calm through fifteen minutes of questioning, and so he could find no reason for doubt or suspicion. In this scenario, Mitchell clearly understood that what he was doing was wrong, because he was able to lie about it to a detective. So he was not insane, for sure.

The trial of Brian David Mitchell began in the first week of November 2010. The charges were kidnapping and sexual trafficking of a minor across state lines, but not rape (perhaps because the punishment for aggravated kidnapping—physical harm or death—is life imprisonment). As he had done in the past, during preliminary hearings in both state and federal courts, Mitchell entered the courtroom singing a Mormon hymn. There were pews for the spectators, elaborate wood paneling on the walls, carpet, chandeliers, and an elevated altar-like bench for the judge. The Smart family, including Elizabeth, sat in the front row, with journalists from around the country filling in the pews behind.

We sat there, in stone cold silence, and listened to Mitchell sing. His eyes were closed. We waited for the judge and the jury. I hate to say this, but Mitchell has a sweet voice, even with some soul. Elizabeth's face was blank, her body stiff. When she was fourteen he sang to her in the foothills—summer nights, looking down on the city and her home. Now she was twenty-three, hearing the same songs in a federal courtroom that feels more like a church. At least it felt like a church to me, the members sitting still and quiet, full of sorrow and fear, waiting for the service to begin.

The judge came in, the jury came in, and Mitchell kept singing, so the judge ordered that he be taken out and put in a room where he could watch the trial on television. In their opening arguments, the prosecution and the defense told the jury that the facts in the case were not in question: both sides agreed that Mitchell had taken Elizabeth at knifepoint and held her captive and raped her many times. The only question for the jury to decide would be whether Mitchell was insane at the time he committed these crimes. In other words, did Mitchell really believe he was the prophet?

The prosecution's strategy was to show that Mitchell could change his persona at will, such as when he was confronted by the homicide detective, and was therefore a narcissistic and sadistic actor who manipulated people in order to obtain sex with children. For instance, they called Mitchell's step-daughter from his marriage with Wanda, and she testified how, when she was fourteen years old, Mitchell cooked her pet rabbit for dinner and fed it to her saying it was chicken, and that he also made her look at pornography while he prayed.

The defense lawyers, who were public defenders, brought in psychiatrists who had examined Mitchell and concluded he was a delusional schizophrenic, an insane man who believed he was talking to God.

The prosecution countered this by calling experts in religion who argued that talking to God is common among Mormons, and therefore normal and not insane. One of these experts, a BYU scholar, estimated that there are at least two hundred men in Utah and the surrounding states who also believe they are "the one mighty and strong."

To counter this point, the defense could have proposed that it's never normal or sane to believe you're the prophet of God, not even for Joseph Smith. They could have pointed out that Mitchell, in his delusions, was emulating Smith, who had two fourteen-year-old wives, among many others. But the defense did not go there, perhaps because the judge and most of the jury and most of the people outside the court-room were Mormons and would have been deeply offended. I think it was also because they knew, after the first day of testimony, they were going to lose.

Elizabeth Smart was the third witness called by the pros-ecution, following her sister and her mother. She took the stand and told the jury, looking straight at them, specifically how Mitchell had raped her that first night, describing how he tried to force entry from above and when that didn't work he rolled her over and did it from behind. Then she told how he made her watch Wanda give him a blow job so she'd know how to do it. She said Mitchell would go into town and bum enough money to buy alcohol and that she'd get drunk just to get through the sex, which was daily. She spoke with a strong voice that never faltered, no tears or sign of guilt or shame, telling the story of her trip to hell and back. After this kind of imagery, the jury wasn't going to care about what Mitchell believed he was doing. The trial took almost five weeks, but really it was over on the first day.

On December 10, 2010, the jury found Brian David Mitchell guilty, without reason of insanity, sending him to spend the rest of his life in a federal penitentiary among other kidnappers, rapists, and killers. Let him sing for them.

Shrapnel
Summer 2002

When you're in a war zone everything blends together—the horrible with the mundane, the threat with the smile, terror with yawns—and you never think about trying to keep things separate. At the end of the day you just want to sleep and there are things that can't be figured out, places you can't go for reasons you don't understand, sentences, comments you wrote down that don't make sense. Things happen all of a sudden and you're either there or you miss it. The only facts are dead bodies; everything else is hearsay quickly becoming mythology.

Later, after you get home, after the jet lag wears off and you stop waking up at 3:00 AM and driving around town, when you can form sentences of more than three words, when you can sit down and eat a meal with other people . . . then the things that happened start to fall in line. You start finding names for things. You write about them, and if you do this well the things go away.

But there are other things you can't call by name and so you can't write about them and they don't go away. They stay inside and you live with them, like shrapnel; your body grows around them.

I interviewed two Pakistani Taliban in the Sheberghan prison whose bodies were littered with shrapnel. One had a bloody scarf wrapped around his head, and the other stood with a stick under his arm for a crutch. Both had torn their clothes to rags for bandages and you could see the pink holes, an inch in diameter, from their chests to their thighs.

A shrapnel wound is not like a bullet wound. A bullet from an automatic assault rifle like an AK explodes the skin going in and coming out of the body and both holes bleed, but shrapnel enters the body red-hot and burns away a circle of skin, cauterizing the edge or rim, and the exposed membrane of muscle or organ pushes up like a pie. It doesn't bleed, and it doesn't easily become infected. The metal fragment either kills you by puncturing the heart or a lung, or it finds a home in flesh.

I was there at the prison to interview men who had, only a few days before, been down in the basement at Qala-i-Jhangi and had survived. I was trying to find out what happened, what it was like to be there, in a dark concrete basement with no light, on a dirt floor, while General Dostum's militia poured in gasoline and diesel fuel and lit it on fire, dropped bombs down ventilation shafts, and then flooded the basement with icy cold water. Somewhere around two hundred men died down there; sixty-seven walked out alive, many badly wounded. These survivors were taken to the Sheberghan prison and stuffed inside shoulder to shoulder with at least two thousand others.

A story was going around among journalists and interpreters that because the prison was full, Dostum was killing Taliban who surrendered and dumping their bodies a few miles away, southeast of Sheberghan, at a place called Dasht-i-Leili. There was talk of mass graves. It was said the Taliban surrendering in Kunduz, a city two hundred miles to the east, were put into metal containers on the back of semitrucks. The doors were shut tight and the men suffocated on the long ride to a hole in the ground. Nobody would go there, no translator or journalist, for fear of General Dostum.

The Sheberghan prison had an inner courtyard, an exercise area, where there were a couple hundred men sitting in groups, walking around; some lay on the ground, wounded. One of those on the ground was a red-headed Circassian with an entry wound in his lower abdomen, an exit wound out his back. He'd been on the open field, a pasture for cavalry horses, when the uprising started. He said the bullet had broken his vertebrae, and standing up was very painful.

"Is it true the Red Cross is outside the gate?" he asked.

I told him yes, they were outside arguing with the guards and making speeches to the press. They weren't allowed to come in.

"Why don't they let them come in? There are no medicines, no change of bandages, everyone's wounds are festering. There is a stench everywhere."

My interpreter, Najibullah's father (who speaks Russian), told him it was "an early stage in the process," and maybe things would get better.

"Later may prove to be too late," he said. "By then foot and arm amputations may become necessary. There is this smell; pus is oozing out of people's wounds."

I asked him why he came to Afghanistan.

"I wasn't allowed to practice my religion at home. I tried to practice and the Russians thought I was with the Chechens. I came here for freedom, as a religious pilgrim, a *mohajir*."

"What do you think about America?"

"It looks like a very nice place in the movies," he said, "but will you talk to someone and get us some medical help? My backbone is broken."

He didn't want to talk about Qala-i-Jhangi.

The guards brought an Iraqi prisoner to me. Or at least he said he was from Iraq. He spoke English and said he'd come to Afghanistan not as a soldier but as a chauffeur, only to make some money to go to school. He'd been a driver for the Taliban, only this. I asked him, on tape, what it was like down in the basement, and he said: It's very problem, this one week. Somebody has died beside you and somebody can't move and says, "Please help me, everybody, my blood is running out from my body." I tell him, "What I help you? I can't move. I can't go outside." And for one week everybody inside not eat anything, and drink water mixed with blood. Water and blood. And you want anything to mouth. You want anything. And you see your friend has died, has died, has died. Now, I want to go to America. I want to complete my life. I want to go to Europe. I don't want to go back to Iraq. I want to go to school. That's my dream.

We spoke with the two Pakistanis last, late in the afternoon, with the guards trying to kick us out. Both prisoners were standing up, although the one was leaning heavily on his crutch. Their heads and faces were smeared with blood and mud and ashes, their bodies pockmarked with shrapnel wounds. I'd never seen even one shrapnel wound before.

"Why did you come to Afghanistan?" I asked.

"Because our mullahs told us to join the holy war against the Great Satan of America."

"So you believe America is the Great Satan?"

"If America oppresses the people, then most certainly America is the Great Satan."

"Would you do it again, would you go back again to fight against America?"

"Yes, if America is still oppressing us, then, yes, we would do it again."

This blew me away. It was late in the day and maybe I was tired, but things started spinning when he said this, that they'd do it again, even though they were wounded and close to death.

"Where are you from?" I asked them.

"From Gilgit," they replied.

"What do you want to have happen now?"

"We just want to go home," they said.

A few weeks later I flew back to the United States and wrote my story, but I didn't mention the wounded prisoners or what they had said about being willing to do it all over again. This became the shrapnel in my body, and the only way to get rid of it was to go to Pakistan, to Gilgit, and see where those two guys came from.

Looking for the Taliban
in Northern Pakistan
July, 2002

The bus station in the old part of Peshawar is like a wasp's
nest made from oil and dirt, with men on bikes and motor-
cycles swarming the hive where the buses rest. I am inside
a bus, looking out at them. They all have beards and wear
pajamas, or *shalwar kameez*, with a white pillbox hat. They
are Pashtun, Afghans. Peshawar is only fifty miles from the
border. I've come to Pakistan to write a story for a men's
fashion magazine, but I have no contacts and no plan other
than I want to go to Gilgit, up north in the mountains. I have
a map and a backpack.

I could have flown to Gilgit from Islamabad, or I could have
gone up the Karakoram Highway, which follows the Indus
River, but I wanted to take this other, more circuitous road
that follows the border with Afghanistan, north through the
Hindu Kush, an area sometimes called Pashtunistan because
here the Pashtuns have never recognized the authority of

any state or government other than their own. Many of the Taliban came from this area, and I want to see the place they call home. The area is open to tourism.

But now I am hesitant to leave the bus. Out there it's 105 degrees and the traffic is maddening, insane. Out there some people probably want to kill me. A few months ago, Daniel Pearl got his head cut off, and his killers posted the video on the Internet.

I tell myself if I can just get out of this city and up into the mountains, everything will be fine. My theory is the higher you go, the friendlier people become. Up above ten thousand feet, nobody thinks about war or killing. So I squeeze out of the bus and through the crowd to the street and flag down a cab. I tell the driver to take me to the press club. There I hope to find a translator.

The driver turns and says to me, in English, "Sir, there is no press club in Peshawar."

"There has to be," I say, "it's the place where reporters go to drink."

"Drink?"

I forgot—there is no drinking in Pakistan.

"Where they have tea," I say, "after working. A club, you know, like for the British."

He doesn't know. The British left Peshawar a long time ago. But surely their better traditions still linger. I stick my head out the window and wave at a guy on the sidewalk. He says yes, there is indeed a press club, the Peshawar Press Club, and it isn't so far away. No problem.

I walk into the club and am taken upstairs and to a large room where a news conference is underway. Twenty-five men with notepads sit around a U-shaped table in front of a full-house audience. I sit down in the front, behind four women. A man at the head of the table is speaking into a microphone in Pashto, so I have no idea what he is saying. Luckily, a young man in the audience recognizes my predicament and sits down next to me.

"Sir, if you like, I will translate for you."

He whispers that the conference has been called by the four women sitting in front of us. They're social workers dealing with Afghan refugees. The man with the microphone is chastising the reporters about the lack of answers for what's been happening across the border in Afghanistan.

"Who assassinated Vice President Qadir of Afghanistan last week?" he says. "Do any of you know?"

Nobody speaks.

"Why are Americans dropping bombs on innocent people, like the wedding party in Oruzgan province?"

Again silence.

"It's our duty as members of the press to find these answers," he says. "In order to stop this violence, we must first know why it is happening." Then he looks straight at me and says, "Do you have any questions?"

"No," I say.

"Why not?" snaps the oldest woman sitting in front of me.

"I've only just arrived," I say. "I don't know enough to ask a question."

This silences the room. I sense shock, dismay, contempt. I am the one to blame, the American, the cause of all this.

The meeting is adjourned.

I've been in Peshawar for less than an hour and already I have some enemies.

The young guy's name is Ahmed (names are changed in this story to protect the identities of those involved). He's very polite and formal, beginning his sentences with "Sir" and "*InshAllah*," which means "God willing." He tells me he's either twenty or twenty-one, as no one in his family can remember for sure. They're from Kabul but left in 1996. His father died of cholera, and as the oldest son, Ahmed's now responsible for his mother, his sister, and a cousin. He says he works teaching English to other Afghan kids for $20 a month. I ask him if he will work for me for $20 a day.

"Sir," he says, "I'll be happy to help you in any way I can, regardless of money. Do you want to go to Afghanistan?"

"No, there are other reporters there already," I say. "I want to go north along the border to Chitral and then over to Gilgit. I want to see this place. I've heard it's open to tourism."

"Other years many tourists go to these places, but this year very few," he says.

"But it's possible for us to go there?"

"By plane or by car or by bus?"

"By car. I'd like to see the mountains from the ground."

"I will talk to some people who know this area," he says, "and will tell you tomorrow."

In the morning Ahmed comes by my guesthouse with his uncle, Hamid, a big man with a serious face. He gets right to the point.

"What is it you're looking for?"

"I was in Afghanistan," I say, "and noticed most of the Taliban come from Pakistan, many from the mountains north of here. In America, we know very little about this area, so I'd like to see it and talk to the people who live there."

He looks me straight in the eye, wondering if I am a fool. He breathes deeply and then asks, "Do you have a *shalwar kameez?*"

"No, not yet," I say.

"Tomorrow I will bring a car and we will go with you as far as Chitral. But now we should go to the bazaar and buy some clothes."

I passed his test, although I don't know how or why. Hamid is a stern man who reveals very little through his expressions.

"Does your uncle ever smile?" I ask Ahmed.

"Sir," he says, "he smiles on the inside."

The cab ride is cheaper with Hamid in the car, and men on the street move out of his way. Ahmed tells me Hamid works for a "businessman, taking care of the house," but it seems he's more of a bodyguard than a butler. He walks with determination, paying no mind to the man missing an eyeball or the guy on the ground moving on all fours. The air smells of shit and diesel exhaust. Women in burkhas touch my arm and whisper a few words. Their palms have intricate designs drawn in black ink. They're prostitutes.

We go into a shop and the clerk lays out four *shalwar kameez*. Hamid points to the grey one. I try on some different sandals, and Hamid says the brown ones will be better for me. And I need a white pillbox hat, same as his, same as everybody's. I don't think this is going to work. No one will believe I am Pashtun, but maybe it's more a matter of etiquette.

In the afternoon I go with Ahmed to the school where he teaches English. It's on the edge of town in a refugee colony—acres and acres of mud brick houses separated by ten-foot-high mud walls, running along a canal of stagnant water. The school has six or seven small, dark classrooms with folding chairs and stools, no desks, one lightbulb hanging from the ceiling, a white erase board and a magic marker. I introduce myself to the class of high school boys, telling them I've come to learn about the Pakistani people.

"But we are Afghan," says a boy wearing a baseball hat with the brim turned backward.

"Yes, of course, I forgot. But you were born here in Pakistan, is this correct?"

"Yes, but we are Afghan," says another in T-shirt and jeans. "Peshawar is an Afghan city. You should know these things."

There is some sniggering. I apologize and say there are many things I need to learn about their culture and history, and that is why I came. They don't let me off the hook. They have a lot of questions.

"Is it true Taliban prisoners are being tortured in Guantanamo Bay?"

"Is it true that Jewish people control the U.S. military? There is a book now in France that says Jewish people didn't go to work that day in New York."

"What is Al Qaeda?"

I tell them I don't know, that I'm not an expert, and that many things will probably always be a mystery, but they should be careful about stories in which one group of people is made to look like animals.

"The Jewish people in America didn't know about the attacks," I say. "They would not have kept it a secret. Just think about it. Did you see what happened?"

Yes, they'd watched it on television, and still they thought the Jews were behind it.

"What about the war?" I ask. "Is it a good thing or a bad thing?"

They all think it's a good thing.

"We like America. America helped us defeat the Russians. Now America is the number one superpower in the world."

"But now maybe we should pull out our troops?" I ask.

"No, no," they say. "If the troops leave, then it will be worse than before. There will be much fighting. General Dostum wants all of Afghanistan for Uzbek people. And Hazaras do not belong in Afghanistan. They are from Iran."

"But they live in Afghanistan now," I say, "and there are a lot of them. At some point Afghans are going to have to learn to live with each other."

"General Dostum is a very bad man," says the boy with the baseball cap. "He killed many Pashtuns."

"I was in Afghanistan last year," I say, "and I sat next to Dostum on a couch in his house."

They are shocked. No one is breathing. Finally, one of them asks for my email address, and we talk about other things.

In the evening, after Ahmed has gone home, I take a cab to the Pearl Continental Hotel, where there's a bar for foreigners. The sun is setting as I arrive and the Pearl looks like a little White House. Last fall the place was packed with news teams from around the world, and the roof became a city of tents and generators and satellite dishes. Then, in late November, all the reporters left for the Intercontinental in Kabul. Now the bar is empty except for the bartender and one other customer.

I sit down next to him, introduce myself, and he buys me a beer. He's had a few already and seems to want to talk. He says he's a civil engineer who's been "in the area" for the last twenty years, but then he asks that I not use his name or describe him so he can be recognized. He seems to know a lot about concrete and bridges, but he's also had some military experience and speaks Pashto, Urdu, Arabic, and Punjabi. I'm pretty sure he works for the CIA, and he's drinking hard because his reports have been ignored by his superiors. He's not happy about the way the war is going.

He says, "These bombings now where we're killing women and children will only make things worse. The Pashtun have no concept of time when it comes to revenge. Do you know about the Pashtun code?"

"Yes," I say, "I've read about it, the Pashtunwali, the way of the Pashtun, thousands of years old. Winston Churchill wrote about it when he was stationed here as a young officer. I have it in my notebook."

> . . . the Pashtun tribes are always engaged in private war. Every man is a warrior, a politician and a theologian. Every large house is a real feudal fortress made, it is true, only of sun-baked clay, but with battlements, turrets, loopholes, flanking towers, drawbridges, etc., complete. Every village has its defense. Every family cultivates its vendetta; every clan, its feud. The numerous tribes and combinations of tribes all have their accounts to settle with one another. Nothing is ever forgotten, and very few debts are left unpaid."

"It might be ten days or ten years or forty years," he says, "but it will happen. It will all come back to bite us in the butt."

"Why do you think we weren't able to catch Osama bin Laden?" I ask.

"The CIA created Osama; they could have destroyed him if they wanted to."

"That's kind of cryptic," I say. "What do you mean by that?"

He looks at his beer for a while and says, "Personally, I think he's dead. He had a bad kidney disease, and without good medical treatment he couldn't have lasted long. But he's like Robin Hood: he will live even after he's dead."

I tell him where I want to go and he says I should have an escape route, like through China, in case things get tight.

"Do you have a Chinese visa?" he asks. "You can get one here in town tomorrow."

"Escape into China sounds like an oxymoron to me," I say.

He looks me in the eye and says, "My advice is don't go. People around here believe the prisoners in Guantanamo are being tortured—weights tied to their testicles and bottles of acid put on their stomachs. For someone here who has a relative or a friend in this prison, you'd be like a gift-wrapped package. And, besides this, the fact remains that there are still U.S. troops in Saudi Arabia, infidels drinking beer and pissing on the Holy Land. This is how fundamentalists see it and it infuriates them."

I look at the wall and say nothing.

"If you do go, you should fly," he says.

"I'd rather drive."

"Well," he says, "if you drive, don't stop in Dir. It's the northernmost tribal area, lots of fundamentalists."

"I grew up with fundamentalists, among the Mormons," I say. "They don't scare me. They usually just want to convert you."

"I'm sorry," he says, "when was the last time the Mormons cut off someone's head?"

I know he's trying to help, but I also know he has to tell me this, like a park ranger has to tell you not to leave the trail.

The car is a 1974 Toyota Corolla, a sad burro with skin of lumpy bondo. Hamid drives, working hard on the steering wheel, snaking between the potholes and oncoming traffic, using the whole road to get out of the city. Hamid is a good driver and by studying his actions, I am able to decipher the rules of the road. For instance, it's very important to drive as fast as possible. Passing on blind curves is expected. Margins of six inches are standard. Horns are used to communicate, but not out of anger. There's no reason to get angry or scared because it's Allah's decision as to who will live and who will die.

> Who are we to intercede with Allah except by his permission? He knows what is before us and what is behind us. He controls the heavens and the Earth, and the care of them burdens Him not.

These lines from the Koran are printed on a CD hanging from the rearview mirror. It's Allah's will that we get three flat tires, but it is also His will that they blow out one at a time, always near repair shops. Surely even our vehicle is blessed, for it seems to run by no other force than divine grace. It is all bone on bone, without dampening or absorption, seals cracked and broken, lubricating fluids bleeding into the dust. The mere fact we're moving is enough to make me want to take some vows. Yes, I even wonder if perhaps we are on a special mission for Allah, and if the weather is unusually beautiful and the corn and tobacco unusually tall and the peasant people unusually happy because He, the one who controls the entire universe, has chosen to protect this vehicle and make splendid its mission.

This illustrious vision comes to a sudden end, however, when Hamid pulls off the road and asks if I can drive. He needs to take a nap.

"Yeah, I can drive," I say, thinking, *How hard can it be?* I've never driven on the left side of the road, but I've been studying the basic motions and intentions and feel confident, as usual.

I sit behind the wheel and move through the gearbox with my left hand and then pull out onto the road. My confidence lasts all of four or five seconds, as I realize that there's very little communication between the steering wheel in my hand and the wheels on the ground. It's like holding a child's toy. It takes a 180-degree turn of the steering wheel to get any response, and then the results are unpredictable—sometimes a sudden leap, other times a slow crawl.

Time stops. Space becomes fluid. Terror sets in.

I see an outdoor café and pull off the road, saying, "This looks like a good place for lunch." I want out of the car and then I need some time to find a way to tell Hamid that it should not be reoccupied.

The tables of the café are under shade trees along the edge of the Swat River. We're in a broad, flat valley with fields of dry brown wheat, and the water is emerald green from glacial silt. The mountains are to the north, a dark wall with twenty-thousand-foot snowcapped peaks. It's beautiful, idyllic. The Swat Valley is called "the Switzerland of Pakistan."

I sit wondering if there might be something in the Pashtun code that equates a man's car with his virility. I don't want to insult Hamid by telling him the Toyota should be towed away. I remember another line from Churchill about the Pashtunwali: A man who knew it and observed it faithfully might pass unarmed from one end of the frontier to the other. The slightest technical slip would, however, be fatal.

I approach the subject with care.

"Hamid," I say, "you are an excellent driver—in fact, you might be the best driver I've ever met—but that car is dangerous. I think there's a good chance we might get hurt if we ride in it any farther."

When Hamid hears what I am saying, he turns and looks at the river and remains silent.

I say, "I think we should maybe stay in the next town and look for another car, one we can rent, and then in the morning we can go on."

Hamid replies, speaking slowly, still looking at the water. He says that in the last town where we had the tire repaired he heard some men talking about me, saying things like, "How is it he is here walking freely when his country is bombing innocent people in Afghanistan? We should fight him with our feet." These comments made him believe that this was not a safe area for me.

"They wanted to kick me, or they wanted to kill me?" I ask.

"Yes," says Ahmed, "perhaps both."

"Is it true that Al Qaeda has offered a reward for any dead American?"

"Yes," says Hamid.

"How much is it?"

"A lot, maybe one million rupees." (That is the equivalent of U.S.$16,000.)

"So why don't you kill me and take the money?"

He turns and looks right at me and says, "Pashtuns don't kill for money; we kill for revenge."

"But do you have family or friends who were killed by Americans?"

"Yes," he says. "My friend and I fought with the Americans at Tora Bora, but they killed him by mistake."

"How often does this happen?"

"Every day."

"Every day?"

"The Americans pay lots of money for information as to who is Taliban," says Hamid, "and some people lie and say their enemies are Taliban, but they are not, they are only the enemies of these people."

"Do you understand this, or are you confused by it?" I ask.

"I understand it completely," he says. "They are killing the tree by cutting the roots."

"Did you ever support the Taliban?" I ask.

"When the Russians left Afghanistan, there was no justice. This is what created the Taliban and Osama bin Laden. He gave much charity to the people. He built tunnels and roads. He was a beautiful man, an angel, and honest. He gave me a cow. But if he were standing here now I would kill him."

"Why?"

"Because he destroyed Afghanistan. He wanted all the power for himself."

"He gave you a cow?"

"Yes, to my family."

The waiter brings a chicken cooked in a red curry sauce, some chapatis, and Coca-Cola in bottles, with straws. We eat in silence, and when we are finished I ask Hamid, "What about the car?"

"We will leave it in the next town, Chakdarra, and take a local car to Dir. We can spend the night there."

Dir. The man in the bar told me not to stop in Dir.

I'm stumped and decide to let Hamid handle things. According to the Pashtunwali, the flip side of revenge is hospitality and protection, so from the moment Hamid agreed to take me to Chitral he became responsible for my safety, and he will sacrifice everything—his land, his money, his wife, even his own life—to protect me. So I go with the code.

Dir is up in the mountains, about eight thousand feet above sea level, only about twenty-five miles from Afghanistan. The air is much cooler here and there are clumps of forests—pine, cedar, and fir—and small hamlets up on the steep hillsides, terraced fields, long irrigation canals bringing water from high up in the drainages. The stream in the bottom of the canyon is clear and would be good for trout. Coming into town, I can smell cedar smoke from kitchen stoves, which reminds me of the mountains of Utah.

Ahmed tells me many men from Dir district went to Afghanistan with the Malakand Division, a force of ten thousand men following Sufi Mohammed, a grey-bearded mullah who swore he would defeat the American forces armed only with an axe. Nine hundred of his men did not come back.

We stop at a hotel overlooking the trout stream and are given the best room in the house, as there are no other guests, but when we get to the room there are four men sitting on the floor and talking. I apologize and say they can stay, that we'll take another room, but the manager insists they leave. They get up and walk out, each scowling at me as they pass by.

Hamid goes out to talk to people on the street, and Ahmed and I go up on the roof with my binoculars to look at the mountain peaks, which form the border with Afghanistan. And then, as I'm showing him how to focus the binoculars, a hand grenade or small bomb explodes in the street in front of the hotel. We look around for cover, but there isn't any. Then another goes off in the same place.

"Maybe we should go back down," I say.

I ask the manager what's going on and he says some men are working on the road, that it's nothing, not a problem, but I don't believe him. He's scared and trying to hide it.

Hamid comes back and says we should sit on the floor and have a talk. He's learned that the four men who left the room are telling everyone in the village that there's an American at the hotel.

"We shouldn't stay here," he says.

"Well, let's not stay here then," I quickly reply. "I don't want anyone to get hurt."

"If somebody comes for you, we will fight to protect you," Ahmed says. "Hamid will defend you with his life."

"Yes, I know he will, but that's just the kind of thing I don't want to happen. If somebody comes for us they'll have guns and we'll be like sitting ducks. You know, ducks? Never mind. Let's just get another car and see if the driver will take us to Chitral."

They don't see that as an option. In one hour the sun will be down and it's still a long drive up and over the ten-thousand-foot-high Lowari Pass. No one will drive it at night.

"Then let's go back to Chakdarra and get the other car," I say.

This doesn't seem like a very good idea to them either. They've been calm up to this point, but now they're scared, frozen, and fear is as contagious as laughter. My chest tightens up so I can only take short breaths. I wish I believed in God, both because I don't want to go out like a light and because then I wouldn't be lying to Ahmed and Hamid. I'd told them I am a Christian, but really I am the worst kind of infidel, and if they'd known this they wouldn't be here, risking their necks to help me.

"Okay," I say, my voice cracking, "let's go now."

Hamid stands up and says he has an idea. He's had "some business" with the "head man" in the village and he wants to go to this man's house and talk to him before we leave, just to get his opinion.

The house is a mansion, somewhat in the prairie house style of Frank Lloyd Wright, surrounded by a twelve-foot-high wall with a steel gate. The front yard has a lawn with rose bushes and three tall pine trees. At the edge of the lawn is an iron fence just before the ground drops away to the river gorge. The view is of the mountains along the Afghanistan border.

The "head man" is about sixty-five years old, with a round belly, the first person I've seen who's overweight. He nearly falls over from laughing so hard when he sees me. I look ridiculous wearing a Pashtun hat and a *shalwar kameez*.

"Hamid tells me you are the head man of this village," I say. This he also finds hilarious.

"No," he says when he catches his breath. "I am the head of only this house, fortunately. What can I do for you?"

"It seems my presence in town has upset some people, and we're thinking it would be better to leave."

"No, not at all," he says. "We have many foreigners come through town. This year not so many, but you are not the first. We have three good hotels where you can stay and not worry, or, if you like, you can stay here as my guests."

I accept the offer. The high wall and the steel gate make the choice an easy one.

"Please, if you will sit and wait, I have some things to attend to and my son is coming. He speaks good English."

Our host, whose name is Khaista-Rehman, speaks with two men on the lawn while we sit on the veranda drinking tea with milk and sugar. I feel a lot better, but Hamid and Ahmed still seem kind of jumpy, perhaps because of the sudden opulence of our surroundings. They sit straight and proud in the lawn chairs, but they are, at heart, poor refugees used to living in squalor.

After twenty minutes, a young man comes through the gate and walks over to Khaista-Rehman to give him a hug. Both Ahmed and Hamid jerk back in their chairs when they see him.

"This man is Al Qaeda!" says Hamid. "This is how they dress."

To me, the young man looks harmless, like a young Cat Stevens with reading glasses. His hair and beard are long and untrimmed, but he's wearing a *shalwar kameez*, the same as everybody, except it's made from hemp. He comes over and sits down. Hamid sits between us.

His name is Haider Ali, and he is twenty-five years old, a university student with a bachelor's degree in anthropology who is working on a master's degree in criminology. He's home for the summer, spending his time making pilgrimages to the mosques up high in the mountains, visiting with the people and teaching the Koran.

"My friends think that you are Al Qaeda," I say.

"And what do you think?" he asks, looking at me over the top of his reading glasses like an old professor.

"I think you and your father are very kind to let us stay here. I feel comfortable."

"There is no need for you to worry," he says. "I wish only to show you that Islam is a religion of peace. How have you been treated since your arrival in Pakistan?"

"So far I've been surprised at how friendly the people are. Everyone has gone out of their way to help me."

"Are you a Christian?" he asks.

"Yes," I say.

"What kind?"

"Presbyterian." I am lying again, but there's no way around it.

"Mister Scott," he says, "you are worried about your safety here in Pakistan, but I'm wondering what would happen to me if I went to the United States for a visit?"

"Dressed as you are now?" I ask.

"This is the way I dress," he says.

"In the big cities you'd probably be fine, but out in the country, in the middle of the country, you'd most likely have some problems. Lots of people have guns in their cars."

"Christian people?"

"Yes, in some places especially Christian people," I say.

I'm impressed. He's smart and seems to have been trained in the method of Socrates. He asks a few questions, in earnest, like planting sticks of dynamite in the foundation of your belief. Also, he laughs. Not uncontrollably like his father, but just smiling and quietly. This is unusual. The men I've met so far are all stuck in a dour funk.

"Have you seen this show, *Jerry Springer*?" he asks. "I have seen it in a hotel in Lahore."

"What were they talking about?" I ask. "Who were the guests?"

"There were women telling their husbands they no longer had the sexual power. They were no longer pleased by them in bed. Do you think this can be true?"

"It's like professional wrestling," I say. "It's both true and not true at the same time."

"Can something be both true and not true?" he asks.

"Have you seen professional wrestling?"

"With the masks?"

"Yes, exactly. They're stories that are true on a subconscious level. They make them up because people want to hear them or see them acted out."

"But why do they want to hear this story, about how the man has no sexual power?"

"They probably wanted to see if the men would fight. Did they fight?"

"Yes, they fought with their wives. Pushing and hitting."

"And who won?"

"The women, they won! The men said they would take some medicine."

"Well, there you have it," I say.

"I think the American people are the craziest in the world," he says. "Do you also believe this?"

"Yes, for sure," I say, "but that's what I love about them."

The sun goes down and lights up a crescent moon and the planet Venus hanging above the mountains. Ahmed and

Hamid go to bed, and Haider Ali and I stay up and sit on the grass, talking.

"What do you think about what America has done in Afghanistan?" I ask him.

"Mr. Scott, how many terrorists on September eleventh were from Afghanistan?"

"None. They were mainly Saudis, but Osama bin Laden admitted planning and supporting the attacks."

"So for one man you kill a whole nation? Is this fair in your mind?"

"I don't think it's fair, but I also don't think fair matters in war. What matters in war is overwhelming force."

"People here believe that Osama is a creation of the United States. He is not a real person, only an excuse they use for this war."

"But I've seen him on television," I say.

"Who made this tape that you have seen?"

The tape could have been faked in a number of ways, but I just don't believe it.

"Bin Laden's family has a long history in Saudi Arabia and the United States," I say. "There's even a bin Laden chair at Harvard University, or there was. I think he's a real person."

Haider Ali shakes his head and says, "People here believe there is a reason for oil. Research has shown that the resources around the Caspian Sea have enough oil and gas for many years. Now the United States will say that there is Al Qaeda in Kashmir, as Kashmir is the only place that touches Pakistan, India and China, and China is emerging as a world power. America dances the world on one finger."

"I agree with you on these things," I say. "The history of this region has always been about control of the trade routes. It used to be silk; now it's oil."

"Mr. Scott, what do you think about what America is doing?"

"I think we should stop dropping bombs and put the money into building schools and roads and telephone systems. These are things we're very good at, and they're the things Afghanistan needs in order to develop and change."

"Mr. Scott," he asks, "why do you think that Muslim people are so slow to change?"

I have to think about this for a minute. Is it a lack of education? Perhaps stubbornness? Something to do with their fear of women? Then I realize it's a trick question.

"It's because Muslim people don't want to change, isn't it?"

"Yes, it's because we do not want to change."

This is the rub, the problem that will not be solved or joked about. I should have seen it coming, but I didn't, and it falls on me like a brick wall. Haider Ali and many other Muslims have seen the shadow of modernity, and they want none of it. What they want is for the entire world to live according to *sharia*, or Islamic law, as people did back in the days of Mohammed. I was thinking Haider Ali and I are not so different, but I was wrong. We come, literally and figuratively, from different sides of the planet.

The next day Haider Ali offers to go with me to Chitral. He has family there, a cousin we can stay with. This sounds good to me, but Ahmed and Hamid refuse to travel with Haider Ali and they're reluctant to release me to his custody. They give in only when Haider Ali swears to Hamid that no harm will come to me. Haider Ali may or may not be a member of Al Qaeda, but he's definitely Pashtun and so he will not go back on his word.

I spend the next three days with Haider Ali, traveling around Chitral and learning about Islam. Haider Ali says Islam is a religion of peace, but it seems more like a religion of rules to me. Five times a day Haider Ali finds a mosque and goes to pray. Five times a day he washes his body in a certain prescribed order. When he isn't praying or talking, he fingers a necklace of lapis lazuli prayer beads and mouths shuras from the Koran. We eat on the floor using our fingers. He brushes his teeth with the frayed end of a stick. All this is written in the Koran, and the Koran is to be followed, verbatim.

Haider Ali asks me if I think I could become a Muslim, and I say no.

"All you have to do to be accepted into the world of Islam is to repeat these words," he says, and then recites an invocation in Arabic.

Again I tell him no, and he drops the subject.

Wherever we go, whether in the mountains or in the town, people passing by look long and hard at the sight of the two of us together. They call Haider Ali a "Taliban detective" and "Osama's younger brother," and say I look like "FBI." It's no problem for them that I might be a representative of the U.S. government, as everyone in Chitral seemed to be very much in favor of the United States wiping out the Taliban, but they didn't like Haider Ali. Chitralis are ethnically separate from the Pashtuns and are Ishmaili rather than Sunni Muslims. They're also in favor of such things as sending their daughters to school and letting their women go about in public without a burkha. They see fundamentalism as a backward and destructive cultural disease. One young man took me aside and said, "Why are you with this man? Everywhere he is preaching. These are donkey people."

At dinner in a hotel Haider Ali starts telling me how he thinks America will lose the war. He says the Taliban can walk for days in the mountains without water and they sleep on the ground with only a blanket, whereas Americans need all their stuff and carry heavy packs and get tired so easily. Plus, he says Americans are afraid to die, and the Taliban are not.

I tell him he's foolish to underestimate American soldiers, and we start to argue like children. This comes to a halt only when a man comes up and introduces himself as a member of the federal police. He shows us his credentials and sits down, opening his notebook on the table. He asks to see my passport and then he writes down my name and my numbers. He asks what I'm doing and I tell him I'm working on a story for a men's magazine in New York City. He asks what my story is about, and I tell him it's about whether this area is safe for tourism. He asks where I'm going and I tell him I'm on my way to Gilgit. He asks Haider Ali if he will be going with me, and Haider Ali says he hasn't decided.

The man leaves frustrated and angry, and Haider Ali is certain he's with the ISI, Pakistan's intelligence service. He's afraid of the guy. He says the ISI, with support from the CIA, was responsible for the murder of Daniel Pearl. He says their mission is to make all Islamic people look like terrorists, thus providing the United States and the western world with an excuse to wipe out the entire religion.

"Now they know we are together and we are friends," he says. "If they think you will write a story about how we are not all terrorists, then they might make trouble, for both of us. These men are the worst kind of criminals."

Things are definitely getting weird, and I'm starting to get paranoid. I'm thinking, "I'm way the fuck up in northern Pakistan, hanging out with a guy who everyone believes is a member of Al Qaeda, and we're being followed by the ISI, who maybe killed Daniel Pearl . . . it's time to get out of Dodge, time to head even higher in the mountains."

In the morning I leave for Gilgit. Haider Ali stays behind because, he says, there are only Ishmaili people in the mountains between Chitral and Gilgit and he doesn't want to stay in their rooms or eat their food. He doesn't like them, and they don't like him, or his kind.

"These people are not Muslims," he says.

So I go on without him.

I hire a jeep, a driver, and a guide who is also a mountain climber and knows the area very well. He and the driver are cousins, and they're Wahkis, from the Wahkan corridor, eighty miles to the north in Afghanistan. And they smoke hashish, which is a great relief after hanging out with Haider Ali.

From Chitral to Gilgit there's nothing but mountains and canyons and rivers and very few people. There are terraced farms along the rivers and streams up to about nine thousand feet, and after that there are herds of goats and sheep all the way up to twelve thousand feet at Salang Pass, the divide between the Chitral and Gilgit drainages.

I ride in the back of the open jeep, standing up holding

onto the roll bar. The sun is bright; the air is clean; the mountains are twenty thousand feet high and capped with snow and glaciers. In the cities, you have to think in terms of ethnic differences, religious rules, and political boundaries, all ugly, man-made things. But up high in the mountains there is only gravity and the weather, and the only lines are the rivers and ridgelines that separate them, and there's only one word, one name that makes any sense—the Indus.

Think of the Indus River as a tree with its base at Karachi on the Indian Ocean and its upper branches reaching to the top of the Hindu Kush, the Karakoram, and the Central Himalayas. It covers everything from central Afghanistan through Pakistan into Kashmir, Ladakh, and western Tibet—all disputed areas because the mountains make the border lines on the map disappear. The real borders are rivers, and they all flow into the Indus.

It takes three days to get to Gilgit, and on the day we arrive the headlines in the papers are about how the man accused of killing Daniel Pearl, Ahmed Omar Saeed Sheikh, has been sentenced to death. Apparently, many people across Pakistan believe that Sheikh, who is Pashtun and is believed to have once been a CIA operative, has been scapegoated.

The streets of Gilgit are full of men wearing many different kinds of funny hats, tribes from all over Central Asia—Balti and Tibetan nomads, Kashmiri and Hindu Brahmin merchants, Hunza and Wakhi, Hazara and Pashtun. Gilgit sits at an intersection of branches of the Indus River. It's the hub between the Hindu Kush, the Karakoram, and the Central Himalaya, and has always been a crossroads for trade and commerce.

We stop at a hotel where my guide knows the owner. They're old friends and happy to see each other, but when the guy sees my American passport he becomes serious and tells us he can only let us stay one, maybe two nights, as word of my presence will get out and there might be trouble due to the death sentence for Omar Sheikh. He says the Pashtuns in town are very upset. I think he's exaggerating until we go for a walk and it's clear from the stares of young Pashtun men that they know I'm an American and they want to kill me.

I have the names of the two Taliban prisoners I interviewed at the Sheberghan prison last fall, and I came all this way on the pretext that I could find their families and get a story. Maybe they lived and made it back to Gilgit, or maybe they died and I can ask their fathers if they think it was worth it. Or I don't know anymore. None of that is going to work because we've got to get out of here.

So I take out my map and study it. I have ten days until my plane leaves Islamabad, and until then I'd like to keep driving around the mountains, stay up high and keep moving. I ask my guide Hussein where we can go and not have problems, and he draws an eight-hundred-mile route heading east across the southern flank of the Karakoram to Skardu, then south and west over the fourteen-thousand-foot-high Plains of Deosai, then back down to the Indus at the city of Astor, near Nanga Parbat.

"There are no Pashtun people in this whole area, at least not until Astor," he says, "and then there are many. It's a place where they train *jihadis* to go into Kashmir. I think as long as we don't stop there, it will be okay, because from there we follow the Karakoram Highway to Islamabad."

"Great," I say, "let's go."

"But in the morning," he says, "before we leave, we should buy some more hashish."

"Excellent," I say, and this is what we do.

Newroz Resolution
March 21, 2003
DIYARBAKIR, TURKEY

The United States and Great Britain began bombing Baghdad
last night. I watched it on television in tea shops on the
streets of Diyarbakir, in southeastern Turkey, with hundreds
of scared and angry Kurds—live shots of buildings exploding in flames, pink and orange clouds of smoke rising up
into the sky, palm trees in silhouette. Diyarbakir is a city of
more than two million people, sometimes called "the capital
of an independent Kurdistan." I came to Turkey about a
month ago thinking I could enter northern Iraq with the
U.S. troops, as this was the planned invasion route, but then
the Turkish Parliament voted not to allow U.S. troops on
Turkish soil. Ninety percent of the people here are opposed
to the war. So I got stuck in a small town on the Turkey–Iraq
border along with about fifty other journalists who had the
same idea. Nobody is getting in this way, and now the war
has started.

By coincidence, today is Newroz, New Year's Day for the Kurds, a tradition from ancient Zoroastrianism. Newroz is the only day Kurds in Turkey can be openly, even blatantly Kurdish and not get thrown in jail. I was on the street by 9:00 AM and saw a couple hundred police putting on riot gear and standing in formation. There were buses and trucks full of people standing up and waving yellow flags, shouting and singing, all headed north. I jumped on the back of a truck and went with them.

Everyone in the back of the truck knew I was an American, maybe because of the Gap hat I was wearing. They were young people, college students, and they were singing when the truck drove up, but they stopped when I climbed on board. It seemed they were afraid of me, so I smiled and tried to talk to them—told them yes, I was an American, but I didn't have any guns, and we wouldn't be dropping any bombs on Diyarbakir, at least not today—and they eventually loosened up and went back to singing.

From the mid-1980s to the mid-1990s there was a civil war between the Turkish military and an armed insurgency of Kurdish rebels calling themselves the Kurdish Workers Party. At first the rebels wanted an independent Kurdistan; then they were willing to settle for parliamentary representation; and then, after more than twenty thousand rebel, soldier, and civilian casualties, the rebels lost the war. The Turkish military now occupies the entire region, tightly controlling the movement and behavior of the local Kurdish people. If someone steps out of line or starts talking about Kurdish independence, they are taken to jail and beaten. It's a police state where everyone is watched, spied upon, threatened, abused—except for today.

The truck stopped about ten miles outside the city at an open field of dirt and gravel where there were two hundred thousand Kurdish people wearing traditional clothes and dancing in front of a thirty-foot-high bandstand with six stacks of loudspeakers hanging from cranes and blasting Kurdish folk music, sometimes slipping into Kurdish hip-hop. Women were dancing arm in arm like gypsies; men danced solo with scarves waving in their outstretched hands. The man onstage was leading a chant, and I kept hearing the words *America* and *savas*, which means "war."

Somebody near the front of the crowd pulled out a Kurdish flag and was chased through the mass of bodies by plainclothes policemen. An officer quickly took the microphone and ordered his men to stop and for the crowd to calm down. There were thousands of soldiers surrounding the rally and a helicopter circling in the air.

I asked a policeman, "What is the crowd chanting?"

"Oh," he said, "they are saying very bad things."

"Like what?"

"Like they are saying they love Abdullah Ocalan and they send their wishes to the island where he is in jail until we find a way to kill him."

Abdullah Ocalan was the leader of the Kurdish insurrection from 1984 till 1998, when they put him in jail, so the crowd yelling his name was a form of protest.

"But," I said, "I keep hearing the words *America* and *savas*."

"Yes," he said, "they are protesting the war, but on this we are all in agreement."

In this way, the day of celebration of Kurdish identity turned into a political rally against the United States and the war in Iraq.

I thought that once the bombing started, the Kurds in Turkey would side with their relatives in Iraq. In the late 1980s, Saddam Hussein dropped nerve gas bombs on Kurdish cities in northern Iraq, killing about one hundred thousand civilians. But now the people here are suspicious of America's motives. One man asked me why it takes five thousand airplanes to get rid of Saddam Hussein. He believed President Bush intends to destroy Iraq in order to occupy the country and take control of the oil fields. Others are confused. They ask me, basically, "What the fuck is going on?" They used to like America. Two days ago they would have done anything to get a green card and go to America and pursue the dream. They'd come up to me on the street and ask me for help.

"My friend works in a gas station in New York."

"I know a man who teaches school in Michigan."

"Is there anything you can do for me?"

They spoke as if they were on a sinking ship and I was their lifeboat. But now the Turkish news channels are spinning our attack on Baghdad as a superpower killing innocent and defenseless people—shots of crying women and children mixed with Enya-like sentimental music. Nationalism and ethnicity are now unimportant. This war is being seen as an attack on Islam.

America. Ah-may-ree-ka. It used to be the most powerful word in the world. It would leave the lips of grown men and their hearts would crack open. It meant hope. But now the word means war, *savas*, spoken with a hiss.

I'm going home. I can't do this anymore. I could get into Iraq by another route, perhaps through Kuwait, but I'm sickened by the whole thing. Our troops are going to end up in an urban war, going door-to-door, killing civilians, making things worse, and for what? And why?

Straight Up the Face
The Wasatch Mountains

December was dry every day, and every night it was windy—sixty- to seventy-mile-an-hour gusts whipping the peaks, big rainbow plumes coming off Thunder Ridge and the Twin Peaks at sunrise. The snow on the ground—four feet that fell over Thanksgiving—had turned into an ugly thing of two layers, the top being wind-compacted and hard, so hard in some places you could stand on it and jump up and down, and so weak in others you'd break through in your turns and drop through two feet of deep hoar all the way down to the ground.

The first week of the month, I went up Red Pine to the Pfeifferhorn. I stood on the ridge, looking down the main chute into Maybird, wondering if I should ski it. It was so steep, like a spiral vortex a thousand feet long, down through a cliff band and out onto the open cirque below. If the slope were to slide, I'd be carried to the cirque and buried there in a field of white granite.

The mountain, the fang of the Pfeifferhorn, was on my left shoulder. The Salt Lake Valley was at the reach of my arm, the Great Salt Lake within a toss of my hat. I could see mountain ranges in Nevada and Idaho, and mountain ranges to the east and south that drain into the Green and the Colorado Rivers. I could see the world—this one, beautiful piece of it.

I thought about going back, skiing down the safer way I'd come up, but it was as if the chute was the whole thing, the circle that needed to be closed, and I jumped into it and skied it as straight down as possible.

It was good for a thousand feet, the surface strong enough to hold my turns, but below ten thousand feet the snow turned mean and corrupt and I kept falling, flying head over heels and face-planting, getting snow down my back and almost throwing up from the shock of it. I was so tired by the time I got down to the river that I crossed it without taking off my skis, going from rock to rock, trying not to slip off.

I wanted to blame my condition on the lousy snowpack, but I knew the truth was that I was just getting old.

The third week of December, I got a letter in the mail from the U.S. Forest Service announcing what it called an "experiment" to be conducted in the central Wasatch Mountains. I read the letter. It was about the helicopter permit.

Since the 1970s, a small-scale battle has been going on between backcountry skiers and Wasatch Powderbird Guides, a company that flies wealthy skiers to the tops of the high peaks in helicopters. You can imagine what it's like to spend four or five hours walking four thousand vertical feet up a mountain in complete solitude and silence, looking down on long, untracked slopes of deep powder, only to have a helicopter suddenly appear and drop off six or eight tourists who ski down and cut up the whole slope right in front of you. Tempers tend to flare. It's happened to me, twice, and both times it made me think of that Bruce Cockburn song, "If I Had a Rocket Launcher (I'd blow those fuckers away)."

According to the Forest Service, "the competition has become very heated and has elevated to . . . frightening levels of intimidation and harassment." There'd been reports of backcountry skiers physically occupying helicopter landing sites, incidents of verbal abuse. There was concern someone would be seriously hurt. So the basic idea of the "experiment" was to separate the two parties—have the helicopters go to one area, the backcountry skiers to another. The letter included a schedule listing the specific areas that the two parties should avoid so as not to provoke hostilities.

The letter, of course, was written with a tone of fairness and balance—"There are plenty of mountains out there, no need to fight over one or two"—but it was this same sense of "fairness and balance" that put the American Indians on reservations. By asking backcountry skiers to stay out of certain areas of public land, the Forest Service was giving the helicopters the right to an untracked slope. The "experiment" was merely the beginning of a paper trail that would eventually lead to an official policy: it was a way to cut up and sell something that was never owned to begin with.

The first day of the experiment was January 4, a Sunday, and the Forest Service had set aside White Pine Canyon for the helicopters. I left the house at 5:00 AM, drove up Little Cottonwood Canyon, parked in the lot by the side of the road, and started skiing up in the dark, hoping to be high in the cirque when they bombed the slope at dawn. They call it avalanche control, as if it were possible.

Hiking up, I was angry. This was a bad sign, which I ignored. I had a plan and I was going to stick to my plan, regardless of what might happen. I was going to hike up the Twins, making a track of zigzags right up the face, and then ski back down, carving many wide turns in the powder, ruining the entire slope for the day's helicopter skiers. And then, at the bottom of the slope, I was going to write "Eat Shit and Die" in big letters in the snow.

Sometime in the night, a cloud had blown over from the south and left an inch of snow at eight thousand feet, three inches at nine thousand feet, and six inches at ten thousand feet. Above ten thousand, the trees stopped and the cirque opened up and everything was blowing from all directions, like a cyclone—another bad sign, which I also ignored.

I could see the top of the Twins another thousand feet above, and it was obvious that no helicopter would land there or anywhere near there. It was too windy. Still, I decided to go to the top of the mountain, and for my route I chose to stick to the original plan of going straight up the face.

As it got steeper and steeper, I started to worry about the snow above me. There was a chance, a good chance, that higher up there would be wind-deposited snow in the chutes. Windblown snow has a much higher density than fresh powder, and it often slides off and carries the whole slope with it. So I changed my course and started a traverse over to a ridgeline, where it would be safer. I had to cross three or four steep and narrow chutes, but they were solid, no problem.

But right before the ridge there was a chute with wind-blown snow. I stepped into it and it felt like pancake batter. My spine went stiff and I thought, *This is not good.* A second later, the whole chute fractured and fell, and I fell headfirst with it.

They say you should swim and fight like crazy to stay on top of an avalanche, and I tried, but there was nothing to swim or fight against. I was tumbling and free-falling through the snow, through the air, although there was nothing to breathe but snow and it packed down my bronchial tubes and stuffed my lungs. I fell accelerating, faster and faster, and the snow was pushing me down, down underneath, and I thought, *How long does it take to suffocate? How dark will it be when I die?*

Somehow, after falling maybe three hundred feet down the slope, I was able to somersault over and get my one remaining ski underneath my body and stand on it and hold a line and let the slide go by me. I stood there with my hands on my knees and coughed up the snow in my lungs in three or four hacks that were like a punctuated scream. I looked around at the blizzard I was in and realized that had I been buried everything would have been snowed over in a matter of hours and my body would not have been found until spring.

I stumbled up and down the slide path, looking for my other ski, feeling very much as though I were in a *Twilight Zone* episode in which the guy is really dead, but he doesn't know it. The wind was ferocious, and it may have been snowing or it may have been that the air was full of snow and it seemed I was again being buried in it, only more slowly.

I calmed down, a bit, and found my ski and thought about continuing to the top, because, after all, that had been my plan, and I still wanted to make my very important point. But then, luckily, I realized I'd already made an important point, which was that I was a suicidal maniac who should immediately get down off the mountain and not come back until I learned how to behave on it.

Driving down the canyon and back into the valley, I noticed that my vision was very sharp, the air was especially clean, and the colors of the clouds and the sky and the city were incredibly vibrant. I stopped to get some coffee at the 7-Eleven and watched the traffic go by on Wasatch Boulevard. Even the cars were clean and shiny and beautiful. I was spooked, but I was still alive, and I knew there'd be another day, another battle with the helicopters, and I decided to go home and work on a better plan for fighting them.

Sunday Morning
2004

My wife kicked me out of the house, for good enough reasons, and now I live down by the railroad tracks. The train horns shake the walls and floors of my apartment. They shake my body, and I'm shaky enough already. When I see people I know in the grocery store, they act like they don't see me. I am a pariah.

Listen, the Prophet speaks:

I testify that we are the spirit offspring of a loving God, our Heavenly Father. He has a great plan of salvation whereby his children might be perfected.

She brought the kids together in the family room and announced that I'd slept with other women, so our marriage was over.

I testify that Lucifer, Lucifer is the enemy of all righteousness and seeks the misery of all mankind.

My three kids hate me right now, but they'll be okay. Or maybe they won't. They used to have a father and now they have a failure.

I testify it is time for every man to set in order his own house, both temporarily and spiritually. It is time for the unbeliever to learn for himself that this work is true.

I remember shaking, trembling, convulsing naked on a futon on the floor of a small apartment in Chicago. Outside it was snowing, big flakes floating down, people on the street below shoveling out their cars. I was shaking because I knew someday I would have to tell my wife about the affair and that our marriage would be over, that it was over already, that it was just a matter of time.

I testify, the righteous will be tested. God's wrath will soon shake the nations of the earth.

It will be the hardest on my son, sixteen years old, middle child between two sisters. He looked up to me as a brave and honest man, and now he sees I am a coward and a liar, and this will haunt him for the rest of his life. I have the same ghosts. Now I have given them to him.

I testify that as the forces of evil increase under Lucifer's leadership, and the forces of good increase under Jesus Christ, there will be growing battles between the two until the Final Confirmation.

In Iraq, white phosphorus was dropped on a city called Fallujah, and there are photos of charred bodies on the Internet. Stories of Marines going door-to-door, killing everyone.

As the issue becomes clear and more obvious, all mankind will be required either to align themselves with the Kingdom of God, or the Devil.

I love my kids. I love my wife. Apparently not enough. I have to stay in town to try to take care of them, show them I'm not going to leave, and that I'm sorry. But I've also got to get out of here, or this place is going to kill me. The train horn is a herd of elephants stampeding through the room.

Human Trafficking in Cambodia
2005

I'm standing in a rice field about fifty miles southwest of
Phnom Penh. The sun is a red ball one foot above the
horizon. The long rice grass is luminescent. It's warm and
humid and the air is ringing with shrill locusts in the trees at
the edge of the field. To my right, twenty yards away, there's
an American woman standing in the rice grass with her arms
folded, one leg slightly bent, and her head down. On my
left, in a ditch beside the road, there's a water buffalo caked
with mud, standing motionless, staring me straight in the
eye. Its eyes are so big and black they look as if they could
stop time. Two men ride by on heavy Chinese bicycles, each
wearing sandals and shorts and headlamps powered by six-
pound batteries slung over their shoulders. Each is holding
a wooden spear against the handlebars. Frog hunters. And
from far away—a mile across more fields and trees—comes
an electric guitar and the bass notes to "Oye, Como Va,"
played karaoke-style. The American woman raises her arms

in the air and is slightly swaying her hips to the music and grinding her heels into the dirt.

Her name is Lisa Miller, from New York City, Los Angeles, Chicago, Cincinnati, and Baltimore. Now she's living in Phnom Penh, working for an NGO on a documentary about human trafficking.

Human trafficking, which used to be called the slave trade, has again become a big business worldwide. Cambodia supplies a lot of slaves, all children, mainly girl children, and many come from places like this—small farms out in the countryside. Lisa is a friend of the people who live here.

The village is made of wooden huts built on stilts, with cows and chickens underneath, pigs in a pen around back, fruit trees, vegetable gardens, marijuana plants. Lots of kids running around. Babies on their sisters' backs. Dogs barking. Mosquitoes.

The men come in from the field and sit at a table under one of the stilt houses. We eat dinner sitting cross-legged. It's soup, made from one of the chickens and some of the vegetables, some noodles and some ganja buds—a specialty for Lisa, who says her stomach has been acting up. The men are joking and laughing, pouring shot glasses of homemade alcohol and making toasts where every glass touches. The two oldest men are in their late forties, and one is wearing a hat with a bald eagle and an American flag. I ask him if the Americans bombed this area in the early 1970s, and he says not this village, but in the mountains nearby there were a lot of bombs.

"And you still like America?" I ask.

He says, "Yes, of course, I fought with the Americans as a Lon Nol soldier."

Lon Nol was the anticommunist leader of Cambodia and an ally of the United States from 1970 to 1975, the period when the United States was carpet-bombing the Cambodian countryside, trying to wipe out the communists. The man with the flag and eagle hat tells me the man whose house we are eating in also fought as a Lon Nol soldier, but he died four months ago from AIDS. He and the other men believe his ghost is still here, that he hasn't left yet. We toast to the ghost and it gets quiet, except for the crickets.

After dinner, we walk through a garden to a small hut made from bamboo poles and thatched palm fronds. It's completely dark inside, but there's the whispering voice of an old woman, like a rock being rolled through dry grass. Also the smell of a dead animal.

Someone brings a light, a fluorescent tube on the end of a long extension cord. The woman is at least eighty years old, skin and bones, lying on a wooden bed without a mattress, blanket, or pillow. Her hair is white and her eyes are moist and cloudy. She sits up and holds her arms around her shins. The toes on her right foot have swollen to twice the size of the toes on her left foot, and there's a three-inch square of skin on the top of her foot that is badly infected, rotting, giving off the smell of dead flesh. Above the infection, the skin is a black flame, turning green and yellow. Gangrene.

She says it hurts. It looks like it hurts a lot.

We're told there's no money for a doctor or a hospital, and traditional ointments and teas did nothing to stop the infection. I have money, enough for some antibiotics, but she doesn't need antibiotics. She needs to have her leg cut off.

Lisa sits down next to the old lady, takes her leg gently in her hands, and speaks to her in Khmer. Lisa knows nothing of medicine, but she does know the old woman is dying—slowly and painfully—and she tries to comfort her.

I'm frightened by the whole thing and turn around and see twelve children pressed together just inside the door, all motionless and absolutely quiet, eyes fixed on Lisa's hands, all wondering if this American woman who is tall and beautiful can cure their great-grandmother. Maybe she has magical power. I can't quite take it and step through the kids to get some fresh air and listen to the dogs bark.

Next door there's another hut, completely empty except for the man right in the center, sitting on a stool two feet from a twelve-inch television screen. He's glued to it, as if manning a periscope. The screen shows new cars and houses with carpet and refrigerators, beautiful people with stylish clothes, women with lipstick. It shows this world, another planet, where there's lots of cool stuff and money, a place where grandmothers do not die in the dark from gangrene.

In Cambodia, human trafficking begins when parents sell their kids into slavery, often for less than $50, sometimes as little as $10. I've been having a hard time wrapping my head around this factoid. People in Cambodia are poor, but there are lots of other poor people around the world who do not sell their kids. Lisa has told me that Cambodian parents borrow money, at high rates of interest, to buy things like televisions, and then they need money to pay back the debt, so they sell their kids. But I don't believe this either.

Maybe the kids want to go. Maybe human trafficking is more like a children's crusade, from the dark farms to the bright cities, from the old world to the new world, driven by desire for the life they see on television.

Or maybe not. Actually, I don't understand it at all.

According to the experts, the causes of human trafficking are exploding populations, increasing power differentials between the rich and the poor, corrupt governments, and failed states. Whatever the cause, the children leave the villages and then they are consumed and thrown away like trash. They're put to work in garment factories and paid 15 cents an hour for ninety hours a week; or thrown onto Thai fishing boats, fed methamphetamine for a few years, and then shot and thrown overboard; or sold into prostitution in Phnom Penh, Taipei, or Malaysia; or conscripted into domestic service in Sweden, the United States, or Saudi Arabia.

People are cheaper now than ever before, and there seems to be an endless supply as well as an endless demand. Nobody knows the numbers. Slaves, unlike guns or drugs, are hard to see and count. "Is this boy an employee on your fishing boat?" "Is this girl a willing prostitute?" "Is your maid free to leave the house?" People lie.

The United Nations claims that every year at least six hundred to eight hundred thousand men, women, and children are trafficked as slaves, but others say these numbers are inflated. None of the experts, however, deny there is a serious problem. And many, if not most, have gone past the point of believing in a solution.

When I speak with Cambodians about slavery, they very often don't know what I'm talking about. They answer questions I don't ask, and I ask questions they don't understand. It's frustrating. Perhaps part of the problem comes from there being no word for "slavery" in Khmer. They have no word for slavery, but there is a word for slave—*khiom*, an old word from back in the days of the god/kingdom. Now the word has a new meaning: it means "I." A young Cambodian artist-historian told us this. Maybe he was stretching the etymology of that word, but it made sense to me.

Americans think of slavery as the practice of depriving someone of their individual rights and liberties, turning them into objects that can be bought and sold. But Cambodians have never had a concept of individual rights and liberties, so how can they be deprived of them? They think, *Of course, people can be bought and sold. It happens all the time. What's your problem?* They think of slavery as cheating, a business deal gone bad—one person lies and tricks another into debt-bondage or work with no pay. And cheating they know very well. They'll talk about cheating all day long—how friends and family have been cheated out of their homes, their cars, and their children. But I don't want to know about cheating. I want to know about slavery. I try to make the point that human beings are different than used cars.

"To buy and sell people, isn't this a bad thing?" I ask.

"Yes, sometimes," they say, "like when the person is cheated."

Here's an example of how the cheating happens: A fourteen-year-old girl is bored with living on the farm in the countryside. She has an older sister who left home and went to Phnom Penh and hasn't been heard from since. The fourteen-year-old girl believes if she can get to Phnom Penh, she can find her sister and live with her and maybe get a job in a garment factory. So she sneaks away and gets on a bus, and on the bus she meets a woman who says she can help. The woman tells the girl she knows a restaurant where they need a dishwasher, and she'll take her there. The girl thinks, great, what good fortune. But the restaurant turns out to be a brothel, and the woman sells the girl for $300 and walks away. The girl, being from a poor farm village and knowing nothing of the world, believes this is a debt she has to pay back. The woman on the bus cheated her, used her like a wallet she found on the street.

Until recently, experts in the field of human trafficking believed that members of criminal organizations came to the villages and recruited young bodies with deceits and lies. They called it "stranger danger." But now they're starting to believe most of the time the young people are tricked into slavery by people they know—an aunt, a boyfriend, even their own mothers. Everybody knows how to do it, and usually people are betrayed by those whom they trust.

Another example: Lisa and I visit a family of Vietnamese immigrants living in a wooden shack next to abandoned railroad tracks on the outskirts of Phnom Penh. Lisa knows the family well because she's been interviewing them on videotape for over a year. The mother has thirteen children, and the father has a bad back and is old and can no longer work. To buy food or to pay medical bills, the mother borrows money from her neighbors at the going rate of interest—20 percent a month. Soon she is way over her head in debt and has no way to pay it off except by selling her two youngest daughters into debt bondage as prostitutes.

The mother has done this before, starting when the girls were about ten years old. Her youngest daughter, Auk, is now fifteen, and her sister, Nee, is seventeen, but neither of them are home because the mother recently sold Nee to a brothel in Taiwan and was getting ready to do the same to

Auk, but she ran away. Now, the mother says she is worried sick about Auk and she promises Lisa if Auk comes home she will never sell her again. She says this because she knows Lisa knows where Auk is hiding.

"I have to help those girls," Lisa tells me when we say good-bye to the mother. "I know lots of young prostitutes in this city, but none of them will talk on tape or be honest about their lives because they feel so ashamed. But Nee told me everything, how she volunteered when she was ten years old to become a prostitute in order to get her mother out of debt and how she feels it ruined her life. I have her whole life on tape, and she gave it to me because I told her that if other little girls hear her story, then maybe they won't end up in the same situation. So now I have to help her. I have to try to get her out of that brothel in Taiwan."

"Where is Auk, her sister, hiding?" I ask.

"She's staying with Nee's ex-husband, Mark, on the other side of the city."

"It's like a soap opera," I say.

"Oh," she says, "if it was only that simple."

We drive over to Mark's house to check on Auk. Mark is an American expatriate in his early fifties, wearing pajama pants with a samurai sword strapped to his waist. He says he's just been practicing some martial arts.

Auk comes running from the house and hugs Lisa and starts to cry. She's a girl, barely past puberty. Lisa tells me Auk is worried about two things—the results of her HIV test, which she's afraid to find out about, and, even worse, that by not going home she risks breaking her "mother-daughter relationship." This is a very old and still very strong tradition in

Southeast Asia, in which girls are taught to sacrifice their own well-being in order to help their mothers grow old and die as peacefully as possible, and perhaps have a better incarnation in the next life. A girl who abandons this responsibility cuts herself off from her family forever. She will live alone and die alone and then spend many rebirths in pain and suffering.

Lisa is more worried about Nee than Auk. Auk is safe for now, but Nee is somewhere in Taiwan working as a prostitute, and no one knows when or if she will ever come back. Mark says he's been to a brothel in Taiwan and the men there are very rough with the girls.

Lisa asks Auk if Nee has a telephone and Auk says yes and finds the number. Lisa punches the number into her cell phone and, amazingly, Nee answers. She tells Auk she doesn't know what city she's in, and that she has to sleep with six or seven men a night, and that her stomach hurts. Auk is sobbing and tells her sister to come home, but Nee says she's not going to come home until the $1,000 is paid back because their mother needs her help. Then they hang up and Auk gets in a hammock with a teddy bear and continues to cry.

Mark tells me he moved to Southeast Asia for health reasons. He'd been living in Florida and had arthritis so bad he couldn't walk one block. So he quit his job and flew to Thailand, where he exercised every day, drank lots of tea, and had a lot of sex with young prostitutes. He says he cured himself in a few months.

He says, "Everybody should have a regular sex life. Jesus, when I was living in the States, I couldn't get nothing. I might go six months without getting laid."

After he was in Thailand for a while, Mark flew to Cambodia to renew his visa and took some time to visit a brothel outside Phnom Penh known for having young girls. There he met Nee, who'd been sold to the brothel by her mother. She was thirteen.

Mark liked Nee a lot, maybe even loved her, so he asked her if she wanted to get out of there and go with him. She said yes, for sure. Mark paid the brothel $1,000 for Nee, and then he paid her mother another $1,500. And then he married Nee and bought a big house and let ten members of her family move in.

Mark says he put Nee and Auk in school and taught the younger kids how to ride bicycles. He took them all to the beach on weekends. He loved it.

"You know," he says, "it's funny. It was like I went through this Lolita syndrome. I was in la-la land for two years. Maxed out all my credit cards. Or, part of it, do you ever do something just because you can do it and you think it's the wildest thing and you want to do it? I mean to buy someone out of a brothel was so wild, something you read about in the *National Geographic* in the Sudan or something."

The thing Mark didn't do, however, was pay the girl's mother enough money to cancel her debts, which, at 20 percent interest per month, grew very quickly. The mother, with her daughters out of the business, had no way of covering her obligations. So she convinced Nee to divorce Mark and go back to work in the brothels, which she did.

Then, according to Mark, the mother tried to steal the home away from him while he was out of town. Then she filed charges against him for pedophilia—sleeping with a girl under the age of fourteen—and that cost him a lot of time and worry and $2,000 to pay off the judge. Still, he doesn't hate the mother.

"She's a fucking bitch, excuse my French, [because] she causes all sorts of problems. She's an evil, evil woman, but I kind of like her a little bit. Even after she took me to court, cost me thousands of dollars, almost sent me to prison for years—when I saw her, I gave her a kiss. Like I said, a flaw in my character."

Mark openly admits to all of this. He speaks as if he has no guilt or shame about having sex with a minor, because in his mind he was doing nothing but trying to help her and her family. And he loved her, maybe; he's not sure. Plus, he says he feels okay about talking because he's been given immunity from prosecution by the U.S. Department of Homeland Security in return for helping them obtain evidence to convict another American pedophile with a much worse record.

The next day we meet with the Homeland Security officer. Lisa has met him before, at Mark's house, but she wants to talk to him again to see if he can help get Nee out of the brothel in Taiwan, so he comes over to her office for a chat. His name is Gary, and he's a big guy with a lot of upper-body work, used to be a cop in Los Angeles. Lisa asks him if he knows other Homeland Security officers stationed in Taiwan, and he says, "Why are you asking?"

"You remember Nee, Mark's ex-wife? She's trapped in a brothel in Taiwan and she needs to be rescued. The men who bought her are criminals and they're going to use her up until she's dead unless somebody goes and gets her."

Gary seems kind of stunned by the request and the serious tone of Lisa's voice and says he'll "look into it."

After a brief moment of silence, I ask him why the Department of Homeland Security is in Southeast Asia tracking down pedophiles.

"Because they are terrorists," he says.

"Terrorists?" I ask, dumbfounded.

"Domestic terrorists," he says with some hesitation.

"Domestic terrorists?" I ask. "I've never heard the term."

And this is the end of the visit. He leaves in a huff.

I don't know what to make of this, and neither does Lisa, but she's pretty sure Gary isn't going to help her get Nee out of Taiwan, now that he's pissed.

"Why did you say that?" she asks me, trying not to get upset.

"I just wanted to know. Don't you want to know?"

"These guys can do whatever they want. They're here because they follow the pedophiles on the Web. They spy on people, and pedophiles are an easy target."

"But they're not terrorists. They don't threaten homeland security."

"I don't care," she says. "He could have gotten Nee out of Taiwan and now he's never going to talk to me again."

According to the United Nations, human trafficking includes the recruitment, transportation, transfer, harboring, or receipt of persons, by means of threat or use of force or other forms of coercion, of abduction, of fraud, of deception, of the abuse of power or of a position of vulnerability or of the giving or receiving of payments or benefits to achieve the consent of a person having control over another person.

It goes on and on, passing through a difficult section about the selling of people for use as sexual slaves and ending with "the removal of organs."

Off the record, a man who works for the U.S. State Department in Cambodia tells me he doesn't know what human trafficking is or how it happens, and yet part of his job is to get rid of it. He says his office has more anti-trafficking money than they know what to do with, and much of it comes from religious groups who are friendly with the Bush administration. He calls it cronyism.

Could "human trafficking" be a ruse invented to fund faith-based initiatives? Maybe our efforts to fight human trafficking are similar to our efforts in the War on Drugs, which have only resulted in more, cheaper, and better drugs. Or our War on Terrorism, which has only produced more terrorists. Maybe it's a business.

The other side of this, however, is that Cambodia is actually way fucked up. Mothers really do sell their kids. Babies are sold for adoption; ten-year-old girls are sold for their virginity; boys are sold to beg on the streets of Bangkok and Saigon or are thrown onto fishing boats and never come back. It happens, a lot, and nobody does anything to stop it. Not really.

Cambodia is the only country in the world with a special police task force to fight human trafficking, and in the four years of its existence the number of arrests for sexual trafficking offenses has increased from forty to over six hundred a year. This sounds like a positive statistic until you realize the justice system in Cambodia is just a pretense for extracting money from the accused, who are expected to buy their way out of jail. A pedophilia rap now costs $20,000. The accused hires a lawyer, from jail, and the lawyer pays off the court clerk, the prosecutor, and the judge. The records of court proceedings, such as the number of successful convictions for trafficking-related offenses, are said to rest in the possession of one man, National Police Commissioner Hok Lundy, and he's not been inclined to release them.

The political system in Cambodia is shaped like a pyramid: the people at the top can commit unspeakable crimes, and the people on the bottom have no rights at all. This is where the slaves come from. Money in the form of bribes and extortions flows upward through the pyramid, and violence comes back down—the cultural mechanism of impunity. In its 2004 report on human trafficking, the U.S. State Department claimed that high-ranking members of the Cambodian government are directly involved in and profit from the sale of human beings. This is a well-known fact among the aid workers involved in human trafficking. Many will tell you that Hok Lundy's wife owns a brothel in Malaysia. These are the conditions under which they work.

In this way, the phrase *human trafficking* becomes a bullshit term, propaganda, a way of labeling something we don't understand in order to throw a lot of money at it while loudly saying we are winning the war against it.

Lisa asks me, "Why do men feel entitled to buy sex? Why do you think you have a God-given right to go to a prostitute?"

"I'd never thought of it that way," I say. "I thought God is against men going to prostitutes, that it counts as a sin."

"Men don't feel any shame," she says. "If you have money, you think you can do whatever you want. Men don't care about the girls, but the girls are ruined for life. Don't you see it's wrong? Tell me how you think it's okay."

I tell her it's not okay, but maybe she's taking things a little too personally for her own good and the good of her video project.

She says, "I bought a spy-cam. I want you to go to some brothels and talk to the men and ask them why they think it's okay."

"What kind of a spy-cam?" I ask.

"It's a cell phone, or it looks like a cell phone, and it sits on your belt. I want you to talk to the men, and I want shots of the girls, to show how young they are. Can you do that? Without sleeping with any of the girls?"

I tell her it will be no problem at all.

The first place I visit is an open-air market for girls called the Chicken Farm. It's outside Koh Kong, a town on the southwestern coast. I go with Mao, Lisa's friend, who knows how to find the place because a couple of years ago he had to rescue his own daughter there by buying her back for $500. His ex-wife had sold her to get out of debt.

In Koh Kong there's a river and a port, with ships coming and going from the Gulf of Siam. The Chicken Farm is out in a field near the river, or that's how I'm imagining it. The night is so dark as we approach that I can't see a thing—no moon, no stars, just the dim outlines of six or seven huts and the doorways glowing red, small shrines lit by candles out front, the smell of burning incense. The girls sit in pods of light from flourescent tubes—six in front of me, eight next door, five across the road. They come from the farmlands of Cambodia and Vietnam, twelve to sixteen years old, all for sale.

"Cheap, good price," the pimp tells me. "You want boom boom, $15. You want take, you keep, no problem. Good price, you say."

The girls don't know I'm not there to buy them or have sex with them, and there is fear in their eyes. I look around and there are no other customers, no men to interview, just little girls huddling together under tube lights on a very dark night. So I tell Mao, "I have some shots of the girls. Let's get out of here."

Lisa looks at the tape, and it's all jerky and dark and out of focus. She says I need to go to a brothel in Phnom Penh where there will be customers, Westerners. The place she has in mind is on Street 63, right in the middle of the city, not far from the U.N. offices and the shopping mall.

So I go there in a cab, in the evening, and it's a building like all the other buildings on the street, a run-down shop with apartments above. A young, skinny man with no shirt and a Band-Aid on his forehead greets me out front and asks if I would like to see the girls. I say yes, and we walk up two flights of steep steps to a room that could have once been a classroom or even a small dance studio.

There are twenty girls, fifth-graders, sitting in chairs in a big circle around me. Their faces are covered with white makeup and purple lipstick. Some, maybe most, are from Vietnam. None are virgins. One is straddling my thigh with her arms around my neck, and I can't look at her and I'm trying not to hear the words she's saying, in English, asking me to have sex with her. The others are laughing and giggling with each other, but when I make eye contact, their smiles turn to fear. They are supposed to flirt with me, but they're not even old enough to know how to flirt and they're scared—scared that I might choose them and scared that I might not and they'll be beaten. At this moment, I would rather be almost anywhere else, even with the dead bodies in the basement in Afghanistan.

I feel like running, but then another man walks in—an American by his dress, early sixties, who looks like he's just come from playing golf. He sits down next to me but does not make eye contact, and at that point I stop breathing. I'm there to observe, but he's there for the real thing and I should keep my shit together and try to talk to him, find out what he thinks he's doing, but I bolt for the door and the girls all instantly freak out and start screaming in terror. They stand in front of me and I have to pull arms off my waist and tear hands off my shirt, and just as I get to the stairs the pimp blocks my way and says I can't leave. I grab him by his arms and hold him out over the stairs and ask if he wants me to let go. This calms him down and I run out of there, demons flying, chasing me out the door.

I go back to Lisa's office and we watch the video, or actually we don't watch it because I had the camera in the pause position. I didn't get any tape. So I tell her what happened. I describe the girls and the guy, and she starts to cry. She's not mad at me; she just can't take it anymore, and she's breaking down right in front of me.

"I think the girls are reptilian," she says. "They use that part of their brain. They're always on the bottom tier, always [have] a pain in their stomachs. You ever been hungry for days at a time? Do you know what that feels like?"

I tell her no, I don't know what it feels like, but I think she's freaking out.

Plates are thrown, narrowly missing my head before smashing into walls and the kitchen counter.

After calming down, she says, "I need something to drink."

Lisa's been here for almost five years. She's made friends with a lot of people—from kids who scavenge the garbage to the bodyguards of the prime minister, from pedophiles to State Department officials—and lately many of them have been telling her it's time for her to leave, if not for good, at least for a while.

Breakdowns must be common among NGO workers and diplomats in Cambodia. They spend their days trying to help people, trying to rebuild the country, and many spend their nights trying to drink and dance away the despair that comes from knowing their efforts are failing. The men often descend into hard drugs and prostitutes; the women become lonely. It's tough—tough to sleep through the hot, humid nights, tough to face the street in the morning.

We leave Lisa's office and get in a cab and go to a discotheque, a hip place with murals of fantasy scenes from a tropical island. There's a dance floor with a mirror ball and strobe lights pulsing to Cambodian disco music, bodies crushed together, writhing like snakes in a pit. Lisa walks into it and becomes one of them. I stay in a booth and lie down, looking over at a glassed-off private room that's dark except for a television on the wall showing a National Geographic program on chimpanzees. There are five or six men in the room, customers, sitting in chairs, and four young women serving beer and walking around in high heels and very short skirts. Two men in suits guard the door.

The men in the chairs look bored and tired, uninterested in the women, and there's a chimpanzee on the screen pounding, pounding, pounding a coconut with a rock. I think it's a female chimpanzee, and it seems she is pounding just to show off to the other chimpanzees around her, as if it's her rock and she is pounding with it and none of the other chimps are going to stop her. She's happy: she has a tool and she knows how to use it.

I look to the dance floor and it is also pounding. Lisa is dancing with two Cambodian women, her friends, who were both sold into prostitution before they reached puberty and now support their large families as paid mistresses to sad, middle-aged Westerners. These women are a success, in a way, but they still call Lisa to borrow money when things get tight.

Lisa is trying to dance with her friends but it seems half the men on the floor, all Cambodian, have surrounded her. I look back to the National Geographic special and the chimp is still pounding. Enough, I get it—chimps know how to use tools. From the stone to the strobe light, pounding, pounding, pounding. I understand everything. I understand nothing. I close my eyes and try to sleep.

Rock the Junta
Burma, 2006

One night in Rangoon I had a hard time sleeping and got up early, while it was still dark, and walked a few blocks down to the harbor along the Irrawaddy River, near the pagoda where they keep a single strand of the Buddha's hair. It's a sacred relic for the Burmese, more than two thousand years old, encased in gold. During World War II the British bombed the pagoda to rubble, but when the monks dug through the heap, they found the hair in perfect condition inside a small box. It was a miracle, and they rebuilt the shrine around it.

There were dogs sleeping on the street as if they owned the place, and a line of thirty or forty young monks walking single file, from tallest to shortest, coming out of the pagoda after early morning prayers. On a concrete runway along the river, men and women were exercising in the dark, doing tai chi and walking backward, listening to the BBC or Voice of America in Burmese on transistor radios. The sun came up dark red and monstrous. The river turned from slate to blood.

I wasn't sleeping very well because I'd come to Burma to see if there might be some hope of a revolution, but people seemed more concerned with making money to buy Game Boys and cell phones than protesting in the streets. They lived under one of the most repressive regimes in modern history, which seemed, from the outside, to be very weak. All it would take is a little push and it would collapse.

The people wanted it to happen, but they just didn't seem willing to do it themselves. I don't know how many men had told me they were hoping the United States would invade. The doorman at our guesthouse said, "I want you to tell President Bush to send his army. They will be welcomed by all Myanmar people. Tell them we have plenty of beer for them to drink."

Along the river there were concrete benches under palm trees, mostly filled by sleeping teenagers, boys and girls, one to a bench. But at the end of the pier six boys sat fully awake, listening to their friend sing and play a guitar. He was maybe sixteen years old and the guitar had an Iron Cross Acoustics sticker on the front. I sat down a few feet away, rolled a cigarette, and listened. The kid had a clear, strong voice, and he was pouring his heart out in a blues song from the Mississippi delta, but the words were in Burmese. They'd been up all night, maybe high on methamphetamine, but their clothes were clean—shorts and baseball hats—and they were polite. I didn't have a lighter, and the youngest boy noticed this and waved to a man walking by and told him to give me a light.

I sat there and listened and started disintegrating. This happens sometimes when I hear American music performed in foreign places. The first time was in the Tiki Room at the Bombay Oberoi, listening to a Bengali sing "My Way." The second time was in a Zapatista village in the mountains of Chiapas, listening to a young woman from Montana sing "Redemption Song." Sadness from knowing America really could have been the light of the world if we just wouldn't have been so greedy and stupid.

Burma is a forgotten country. You might have a hard time finding it on a map, and it may not even be called Burma on the map you're looking at. It might be called Myanmar, its official name. It's an extremely poor country, the size of Texas, located between Thailand and India, south of China. For the past forty-four years, it's been cut off from the rest of the world by a junta of xenophobic and superstitious generals calling themselves the State Peace and Development Council. Others call them hungry ghosts.

The population is fifty million, and they live like imprisoned children with very little knowledge of their own history and very little opportunity to learn. Their government controls nearly every aspect of their lives—what they can read, what they can say and think, where they go, how they make money. Nothing much comes into the country, and nothing much goes out—except opium, teak, and jade by way of the black market, which is controlled by the military. Strangely, the country is open to tourism, but not many people care to visit.

I lied on my visa application, saying I was a college professor; my travel companion, Lisa Miller, wrote in "Spiritual Adviser," partly as a joke and partly because we were, as tourists, supposed to be visiting the Buddhist temples that dot the landscape. The country is sometimes called the Golden Land because the bell-shaped pagodas are usually covered in gold paint.

Before going to Burma, I'd read how in 1988 the people had turned out in the streets en masse shouting *Dee-mo-kra-cee!* This protest ended with three thousand people shot dead in the street by their own military. A couple of weeks later, Aung San Suu Kyi, the daughter of the founding father of Burma's democratic movement, made a speech from the steps of Shwedagon Pagoda in Rangoon calling for a second Burmese revolution, and she's been under house arrest pretty much ever since—even when she won a national election in 1990, making her the rightful leader of the country; even when she was awarded the Nobel Peace Prize in 1991.

She lives in her father's house on the shore of a large lake in Rangoon, with guards outside her gate. They do not allow her a telephone or a TV or a radio. She has no mail coming in or going out. In the day, she hears the distant roar of traffic; at night there are frogs. She meditates, a lot. She is, by far, the most powerful person in Burma, but she has no way to speak to her people.

I expected to see a military presence on the streets in Rangoon, the capital city, or what used to be the capital city until late last year when the astrologer of the chief hungry ghost, Chairman Than Shwe, foresaw that it would be prudent to move all government offices four hundred miles north to a small city where they could be located inside a defensible wall. I expected to see tanks shaking the ground or soldiers inside bunkers at the intersections or checkpoints and roadblocks . . . something demonstrating who was in control and who was not. Up in the mountains, the Burmese military was busy burning tribal villages to the ground, systematically raping women, and forcing hundreds of thousands into slave labor camps. But in Rangoon it took two days to even see a policeman—and then they were only traffic cops dressed in white coats and white British Raj helmets, armed only with whistles. Traffic became gridlocked and no one even honked a horn.

And the people on the streets, who I imagined would be huddling and scurrying about like caged rats, seemed instead to be calm and even happy, strolling along, the men sashaying in long skirts and sandals, some sitting on the broken sidewalks in little kindergarten-size plastic chairs, drinking tiny cups of tea. Some of the women smeared light brown cellulose paste in circles on their cheeks, which looked sort of exotic, but is actually a traditional way to protect their skin from the sun.

At one of the busier intersections downtown there was a government billboard that said, in English:

PEOPLE'S DESIRE
—Oppose those relying on external elements, acting as stooges, holding negative views
—Oppose those trying to jeopardize stability of the State and progress of the nation
—Oppose foreign nations interfering in internal affairs of the State
—Crush all internal and external destructive elements as the common enemy

But up above the billboard, on the rooftops of the apartment buildings, there were fields of satellite dishes gazing up to the sky like sunflowers.

It didn't make sense. Inside their homes, people were watching CNN, BBC, HBO, and MTV, while out on the street they were supposed to be wary of stooges.

Everywhere we went, we were watched—long, intense stares coming from every direction, and some of these people laughed at us. Yes, a mockery, seconded by legions of squawking crows in every tree.

Actually, the Burmese people were not all unfriendly. Men would come up to us, trying to sell us shoes and postcards, offering to change money, always some kind of business. We'd try to talk to them. They could ask us where we're from, where we're planning to go, what hotel or guesthouse we're staying at, but it was always a pretend conversation. The minute we'd ask a question about their lives, like "What's it like to live here?" the response would be the same—first a turning away, moving the body and the head to the side, then a glazing over of the eyes, a gaze without focus. They turned inward, pulling a shell around their bodies.

"It is dangerous for us," one man said. "There are spies everywhere."

He was a young social worker for the government, out drinking whiskey with two friends in Rangoon's Chinatown.

"Everyone in Myanmar has either gone to jail or knows someone who has gone to jail for saying the wrong thing," he said. "I have a friend in Insein [pronounced like 'insane'] Prison who held up a sign at a protest. The sign said only one word, 'Democracy.' His sentence is seven years."

Even other Western tourists spoke in whispers, turning in all directions to see if anyone was listening. This syndrome has a name among foreign diplomats and NGO workers— "Burma Head."

In *Discipline & Punish: The Birth of the Prison*, Michel Foucault discusses the social effects of surveillance, using a prison designed by Jeremy Bentham in 1787 as a model. It's called the Panopticon. The cells are arranged in a circle around a central observation tower so that one person inside the tower can see into every cell at all times, but the prisoners, while able to see the tower, never really know whether there is a person in there watching them or not. The observer can see out, but the observed can't see in.

The major effect of the Panopticon is to induce a state of conscious and permanent visibility that ensures the automatic functioning of power. Foucault said that the perfection of power should tend to render its actual exercise unnecessary, that the inmates should be caught up in a power situation of which they are themselves the bearers.

This was why there was no visible military presence in the city. It wasn't necessary. The people controlled themselves. Even tourists were not immune. The effect was a deadening of desire, a flatlining of curiosity and humor, and loneliness hung in the air, heavy as the smog cloud that covers all of Asia. There was not a buzz or a whir or a whisper of testosterone among the men, and the women, although many were beautiful, had not a bit of glamour, not a hint of sensuality among them. The food was horrendous, cooked in the morning and left to sit through the day at room temperature, so that by dinner the stuff on the plate looked like brown entrails and tasted like pure MSG.

And while there was a lot of American music being played all over town, most of it was awful. For instance, we were on a bus that played a video of a girl dressed like Britney Spears but standing stiff as a board and singing the theme to *Flashdance*, only with Burmese lyrics. Behind her on the stage was a large photograph of Mother Teresa, and every time the music came around to the refrain ("She's a maniac, maniac on the floor . . .") the girl would turn to Mother Teresa and sing to her.

This is how it went the first few days in Rangoon. Lisa was getting antsy, wanting to go somewhere or something, anything, to happen.

"The whole country can't be this boring," she said one night as we sat outside our guesthouse, smoking cigarettes. "It makes me want to shoot heroin, and I hate that drug."

The next day we went to church. There was a Baptist church across the street from the Sule Pagoda, pretty much in the center of the city. It seemed strange the junta wouldn't allow democracy but did allow evangelism, and I wanted to check it out.

There have been Baptists in Burma since the early 1800s, when an American missionary named Adoniram Judson built the first church and translated the Bible into Burmese.

This church was packed and stuffy, and the service was pretty much what you see in the States—the same ceremonies and tone of voice in the sermon—but the hymns sounded like a cross between Navajo Pentecostal and Sacred Harp shape note singing, songs going on and on through ten verses and approaching trancelike rhythms.

When we came out of the church the sun was going down and the sky was turning orange and red. Across the street, the spotlights were coming on and illuminating the golden dome of Sule Pagoda.

"You know," Lisa said, "Buddhists pray and meditate alone, but Christians do it together, in a group, and I think this is why people here become Christians. Did you see how they stood up and sang those hymns in there? They were really into it, not at all like the solemn and glum singing in the churches my parents dragged me to as a kid. There was a lot of energy in there."

Before I had time to agree with her, a young man about eighteen to twenty years old came walking by, carrying a guitar. He had long, straight hair down to his shoulders, a little goatee under his chin, and a gold ring in his ear—a hipster. Lisa instantly became his groupie and asked him to play a song. He smiled and spoke just enough English to say he didn't know how to play; he just liked carrying the guitar around.

I asked him what music he liked to listen to.

"Chit San Maung," he said, "number one guitar in Myanmar. Iron Cross, number one band."

"He lives here, in Rangoon?" I asked.

"Yes, he lives here. All Iron Cross live here."

"We want to find him," Lisa said. "We need to talk to him. Do you know where we can find him?"

"No," the kid said, and then smiled and walked away.

I guess we hadn't been paying attention all that well, because now we started seeing Iron Cross bumper stickers on a lot of the beat-up taxicabs around the city. Sometimes the cabs had one kind of bumper sticker that read, in English, "Drive Safely." But the other kind of sticker was either "Iron Cross Acoustics" or "Iron Cross Unplugged."

Also, we started seeing more teenage boys with guitars—sitting in doorways or outside apartment buildings, strumming, trying to learn how to play. They all knew Chit San Maung. One kid said Chit was "the best guitar player in all of Asia, no question."

We heard Iron Cross songs in taxicabs, coming out of apartment windows, and from large speakers set up on the street by kids selling sunglasses. Some of it sounded like Metallica; some of it sounded like Hawaiian cowboy music. All the songs were covers, but the lyrics were always in Burmese.

We were in a coffee shop for tourists, and Iron Cross was performing live on television. The sound was off, but the band was into something loud and fast. The singer had a shaved head and was screaming into the microphone, the drummer was in a frenzy, and Chit San Maung—who looked like a friendly headhunter—was ripping up some meat on his guitar, sticking it to the man.

It seemed strange these guys were not in jail.

The next morning we were both sick, coughing up yellowish green phlegm, so we took a taxi to a health clinic inside one of the more expensive hotels in town. (Burma has close to the lowest health care standards of any country in the world.) The driver had an English-Burmese dictionary on the dashboard and wanted to talk. He said he'd grown up in a village in the mountains along the border with Thailand, but his life there was so boring he left and came to the city to seek his fortune.

"I have not one good thing to say about government," he said. "They ruin my country. They lie about everything. Nobody knows the truth. We cannot. Have you seen our newspaper? Only good news. All a bluff. First thing children learn in school is not ask questions. At university you pay for grades; nobody learns; nobody knows how to make what we need. We export rubber; we don't know how to make tires. When we buy them, very expensive."

"Could you leave the country if you wanted to go?" I asked.

"Yes, we can go out. If we have money, we can go out, but I don't have money. Only military, black market men have money."

"But if you could leave, would you stay away or would you come back?"

"I love my country, you understand? I want to die in my country because I love my people. If government says we live on 500 kyat (50 cents) a day, we live on 500 kyat a day, okay. We can do this and be happy with each other, love each other. But this government is very bad men."

"Do you know the band Iron Cross?" I asked.

"Yes, my friend is friend with Chit San Maung, guitar player."

By the time we came out of the clinic with some antibiotics, the cab driver had Chit's phone number. I called Chit and he spoke enough English to understand what I was asking. Mainly he said yes, yes, yes, and that he'd send a car to pick us up.

The car came at eight in the evening, a new black Land Cruiser with tinted windows and some bumper stickers I hadn't seen on any other car—"No Jesus, No Peace. Know Jesus, Know Peace," "Never Say Die," as well as "Iron Cross Acoustics"—the name of their new album.

I asked the driver if Chit was a Christian, and he said, "Yes, for sure."

"So are Iron Cross songs religious songs?"

"No," he said, "it's not allowed. No words in English, no Christian words. Only love songs."

Then he stuck in an Iron Cross CD and turned it up loud, maybe to get me to stop asking questions, maybe because it was a beautiful song.

The boulevards in Rangoon are lined with palms and banyan trees. It's not a bad city, the way it's laid out, and it's better at night, when we're weaving through traffic at forty miles an hour, listening to a song that sounds like a train coming down the tracks while passing buses packed tightly with people, arms and heads hanging out the windows, flying by frog-legged men pedaling tricycle rickshaws, too fast to see strange animist shrines with Christmas tree lights or a karaoke bar with women modeling onstage.

Chit's house had a wall around the outside and a sign out front that said "PTL Digital Studios." I asked the driver if PTL stood for "Praise the Lord" and he said yes. But when I asked him if he'd heard of Jim and Tammy Faye Baker, he said no.

Downstairs there was a small recording studio—a sound room with a double-paned window separating it from the control room. We were taken up two flights of stairs into the production room—carpet on the floor, a large computer and big speakers sitting on a desk, ten guitars hanging on the wall, Iron Cross concert posters, including one from their 2003 tour to America.

Chit came in and shook our hands, and he was like a 130-pound lightbulb, so happy we'd come. He was with an older man he introduced as his uncle who, he said, was going to help translate. He didn't look like Chit at all, more like a wise-guy type, but at the time I just accepted the thing without question.

Chit said he'd started playing in church when he was eight years old. The church had a good choir and they sang "Amazing Grace," things like that, and he also had a Chet Atkins tape that he listened to a lot. When he was a teenager, he moved to Rangoon and studied with the most famous guitar player in the country at that time. He was the one who came up with the name Iron Cross to show respect, Chit said, for the World War I German medal for heroism, bravery, and leadership.

I asked him where they played in the States, and he said New York, Washington, D.C., San Francisco, and Los Angeles.

"Have you heard of Jim and Tammy Faye Baker?" I had to ask.

"No, who are they?"

"Oh, just a couple who had a TV show in America called *Praise the Lord*. It doesn't matter. Your driver told us your songs aren't religious, that the government won't allow it."

"Yes," he said, "we give them the words and if they don't like them they write new words."

"Does that bother you?"

"No, they do their job; we do ours. We only play love songs, and sometimes it's hard to say who writes the words. Sometimes the words are not important."

"You know, the first time we saw you was on TV and the sound was turned off so we couldn't even hear the music, but I saw you have power in your guitar. It was obvious, just in the way you were playing, and I wondered why you weren't in jail. Why does the government let you play anything at all?"

Up to that point he had understood my questions and answered them by himself, but suddenly he pretended he didn't understand the question and turned to his uncle for help. They talked for a minute in Burmese and then the uncle said, "Iron Cross songs are not about politics."

163

"But," I said, "have you seen *Woodstock*, the movie of the concert?"

Chit nodded his head.

"There's a part where Jimi Hendrix . . . you know Jimi Hendrix?"

Another nod.

"There's a part where Jimi Hendrix plays the 'The Star-Spangled Banner,' our national anthem, only he tears the hell out of it, makes it burst into flames, and this was during the Vietnam War."

Another nod, only barely.

"Could you play like that and not get busted?"

By that time Chit was turning around and looking at his uncle. Then he grabbed his cell phone from his pocket and looked at it as if it had gone off, even though it hadn't, and he excused himself and left the room.

I felt so stupid. I was talking to him as if he were a rock star in America, immune from prosecution, thinking his uncle really was his uncle and his friend. But his "uncle" was a spook, there to monitor the interview, for sure.

So we sat in silence for a minute with the uncle, and then Lisa tried to break the tension by asking him if he meditates.

"Yes," the uncle said, "more when I was younger than now. Now not as much as I would like."

"I'm the same way," she said. "I used to do it every day but now it's like I have to go on a retreat or something."

"Meditation makes you free," he said. "No worries, no anxiety."

"See?" she said to me. "You should meditate. It would make you less crazy."

And I must have been crazy because I just couldn't shut up. I asked the uncle, "Do you know what I'm talking about? Do you understand what I'm saying about the guitar?"

"Yes," he said, "I think it sometimes might be true, but what you say will not happen here. People listen to Iron Cross to be happy, to forget their lives. They gamble on football, English Premier League, for the same reason. It's a diversion."

"So you don't see another rebellion coming, like what happened in 1988?"

"No, people are busy finding money to buy things they want. Boys today want to fight in video games, not in the street."

"Then what can help?"

He thought for a minute and said, "I'm afraid nothing can help this."

Chit came back in the room, apologized again, and sat down. There were beads of sweat on his forehead and his light had gone off. I'd blown it out. The interview was over. But as we were leaving, Chit said Iron Cross was going to play on Friday in the park, outdoors, and if we wanted to come he'd have some tickets brought by our guesthouse.

The band was under pressure from the government, because you can't play rock and roll, even with love song lyrics, without at least acting like you're challenging the status quo. And there had been incidents. The first happened in 1995 when the band's lead singer, Lay Phyu, came out with a solo album titled *Power 54*. The title was approved by the censors and the CD was on the shelves in the stores before the authorities realized that *54* is Aung San Suu Kyi's address on University Avenue in Rangoon.

The government sent men out in the streets with bull-horns demanding that anyone with a copy of the CD bring it out and hand it over so that it could be burned. They called Lay Phyu in for a meeting, whereupon he insisted that the name had nothing to do with Aung San Suu Kyi; it merely connoted the number of songs produced by Iron Cross to date, nothing more, and if they wanted he would change the name to *Power*. Iron Cross was banned from performing for a period of time—I don't know how long—but Lay Phyu didn't stop causing trouble.

His hair reached his waist and the government told him to cut it, so he shaved his head. Iron Cross was asked, or ordered, to perform at the wedding of a military officer's son, but Lay Phyu refused, saying, "These are not our people." Lay Phyu was a rebel and very popular among the poor as well as the sons and daughters of the military junta.

The poor, however, did not make it to the concert. It was in a large park, by a lake, with lots of big trees. The tickets cost $4, the beer $1. A schoolteacher or a lawyer in Burma makes $16 a month, so the four thousand young people who came were all upper class.

Boys arrived with boys, girls arrived with girls, and there was very little interaction between them. About half the boys were dressed conservatively in button-up shirts; the other half, the hipsters, wore T-shirts with dragons or Nirvana on the front, blue jeans, chains hanging from belts, necklaces, earrings, sneakers. The girls were pretty much covered up. I saw three in short skirts and tight shirts and two in dresses and high heels, but that was about it for the fashion show.

The band came out and launched into a cover of a song I'd heard before but couldn't name, maybe Nine Inch Nails or Metallica. The hipsters danced with their hands in the air; the others stood motionless. No women danced.

Lay Phyu wasn't there, and when the song ended some of the crowd started chanting, "Lay Phyu! Lay Phyu! Lay Phyu!"

But he didn't come out, and the band played another cover of a song I'd heard before but couldn't name, and then there was more chanting of "Lay Phyu!" Still no Lay Phyu.

I asked the guy next to me what was up, and he said Lay Phyu had been banned from performing. It had happened recently and everyone there knew about it.

I wanted the revolution to start right there, but the band played on and the crowd forgot about Lay Phyu. The hipsters got drunk and danced with their shirts off, tattoos bared, thrashing around in a mosh pit–type thing, getting more and more crazy, shaking their long hair and screaming out the words to the songs. Everybody knew the words to the songs, and as the night went on the band slowed down and it became kind of a group singalong, the same thing we'd seen in the Baptist church.

When it was over, it was over. No encores, no lighters. The crowd left as one great mass, as though they thought there would be trouble if they stayed, or they didn't want to be seen as individuals. Strength in numbers, even when running away.

We ended up in a cab with the three girls in short skirts in the backseat. Two of them spoke nearly perfect English, which I thought was a stroke of good luck, but when I asked them "What's the deal with Lay Phyu?" they shut up and didn't speak a word until they got out of the cab at their apartment building. It was one quiet taxi ride, for sure.

People wouldn't talk about it, and those who did gave me four or five different answers: He was caught gambling at his house; he got into an argument with someone else in the band—an ego thing; he was a drug addict; and . . . he'd been out of the country and recorded a song that was critical of the government and they finally found out about it. Nobody knew for sure, and this was okay with them.

But it was not okay with me. It pissed me off. If they didn't care what happened to Lay Phyu, then I found it hard to care about them. If you don't care, then it's not rock and roll. If you don't care, it's not even music. When Lay Phyu didn't come out at the concert, the audience should have destroyed the stage. The Burmese people should not wait for the United States to send our troops, and they should not wait on the UN Security Council to approve a resolution. The Burmese people need to start the revolution themselves, as they did in 1988.

Listen: Aung San Suu Kyi is meditating on her back porch beside the lake. Sitting on a cushion in lotus position, she empties her mind of thoughts and desires. She is not a prisoner. A frog plops in the water.

The Source of the Spell
The Avenues, Salt Lake City

It's the spring of 2009. I just bought a house. I just lost my girlfriend. I've been trying to write about Captain John Gunnison and how he and his men got massacred in central Utah in 1853, some say by Indians, some say by Mormons dressed as Indians.

In 1852, Gunnison published a history titled *The Mormons or Latter-Day Saints, in the Valley of the Great Salt Lake: A History of Their Rise and Progress, Peculiar Doctrines, Present Condition.* It was generally complimentary of Mormon people but critical of their religion. For instance, Gunnison called Mormonism "an unfortunate mistake" and said Joseph Smith amounted to nothing more than a con man. When the massacre happened, many people in Salt Lake City and across the nation believed it had been ordered by Smith's successor, Brigham Young, as revenge for what Gunnison had written in his book.

I wanted to buy a house because I was afraid we, as a country, are entering a bad time when it's best to hunker down and hold on. I qualified for a loan because two years ago I took a job as a full-time professor at a state university. But my girlfriend, Lisa Miller, didn't want anything to do with owning a house. She wasn't ready for the commitment, said she needed another year.

I told her now is the time. I said, "America is going down the tubes and through the wash. Pretty soon there's only going to be two types of people—those who have a home, and those who do not. This is a good house, something we could fix up and either live in or sell for a profit."

She said no.

I didn't believe her.

The reason I was trying to write about John Gunnison had to do with his advice on dealing with the "Mormon problem." In the early 1850s, nearly everyone in the country was worried about the Mormons and how they were building a god/ kingdom in the Great Basin. And they were polygamists. Gunnison, who'd lived among the Mormons and studied their history, said the best policy was to "leave them severely alone," as persecution would only make them stronger.

I remember watching the World Trade Center towers fall on 9/11 with my young daughter. I was at work and she called and said everyone was sent home from school because planes were flying into buildings in New York City. I drove home and we watched the buildings collapse on television. I told her everything was going to be different now because the United States would respond with military force, and this would only make things worse, for a long time, maybe her whole life. I'd read Gunnison's report and I knew what he said about the early Mormons could also be applied to

Muslim terrorists—persecution, military force, would only make them stronger.

Now, in mid-2009, our military efforts in fighting the War on Terrorism have thus far only created more enemies who pose a greater threat to our security. We have made the problem much worse, at a great expense in lives and money and fossil fuels. I haven't met anyone yet who argues the point. The response is typically: "Well, what else can we do? They attacked us."

There's a poem by Goethe, adapted by Disney in *Fantasia*, about the sorcerer's apprentice. The apprentice casts a spell on a broom to make it his slave. The broom sprouts legs and arms and starts carrying water into the sorcerer's castle. Seeing his work is being done, the apprentice takes a nap, only to wake up and find the castle flooded. The broom has carried way too much water, and it won't stop. The apprentice freaks out and uses an axe to chop the broom into little pieces, trying to kill it, but then each little splinter grows into a new broom that carries water, twice as fast. It's frightening. Our situation with the terrorists is like this, only we don't have a sorcerer, like the one in the poem, to reverse the spell.

When I first met Lisa, I felt like a moth flying into a light. She was beautiful and funny and alluring in a way I'd never seen before, as if she had no fear of life or its painful consequences. We traveled and worked on stories together, around the United States and the world. I paid for everything, and every time, every trip, I lost money. It was a downward spiral. Still, I couldn't stop taking her with me because I was in love with her, and when I was with her other people were not afraid of me. Doors opened to her charm.

Traveling with Lisa should have been more fun than I could imagine, but I just couldn't lighten up. She was looking for enlightenment, prone to losing herself in the moment and falling in love with whomever we met, but I had a deadline and expenses and I needed a story, not satori. And I'd get jealous of her friends, mainly her male friends, and she had a lot of them, all over the world.

My new house is actually very old, more than one hundred years old. It sits on a hillside on the north end of the Salt Lake Valley in a neighborhood called the Avenues. During the recent two-year slump in housing prices, homes in this zip code have lost the least value of any in the state of Utah. It's the best place to live if you want to be close to downtown and the university, and the view of the valley and the Wasatch Mountains is sometimes breathtaking. I sit on my front porch and wonder if the Mormons are right and this *is* the promised land.

Fifteen thousand years ago, the Salt Lake Valley was covered by a vast inland sea, one thousand feet deep, the size of Lake Michigan. The people who lived here then hunted megafauna like wooly mammoths and thirty-pound trout. They were "hunters and gatherers," a term used by anthropologists to describe the type of culture common to human beings for about 99 percent of our history on the planet, much different than our culture today. For example, in the worldview of the hunter and gatherer time was circular, not linear. In their lives the things that had meaning were things that repeated, over and over, like the seasons, transcendent of history. Things happen because they have always happened and always will happen. But modern civilization is all about history, a straight line instead of a circle. Things happen once and everything changes from there, usually for the worse, all heading to the Apocalypse.

Another thing that was different about hunters and gatherers was that they didn't own their land. They had a concept of territory, which was their turf, their hood, and it included the natural and supernatural, animals and spirits, but they didn't have written title to it.

Lisa wanted out of our culture and into this primitive world. She would build altars and pray to spirits and read the tarot. She wanted to go to seminars on shamanism and yoga retreats. I told her I didn't believe in that stuff and just wanted to work. I'd remind her that in order to keep going, we needed to make money. I had to live in the world of timely monthly payments.

The Salt Lake Valley first became property in the year AD 1540, when Hernando de Alarcón sailed to the mouth of the Colorado River and with a wave of his hand proclaimed the river and all its tributary lands the dominion of God and the King of Spain. The Native Americans, ancestors of modern-day Pimas, looked upon Alarcón and his twenty men with wonder and awe, stroking their blond hair, pinching their bodies.

Alarcón wrote, The natives "took corn and other seeds in their mouths and sprayed me with them, saying that was the kind of offering they made to the sun." He told them there was a God in heaven and that his name was Jesus Christ and that he saved us all one day by dying on a cross. He asked the natives to gather sticks, and then they made thousands of crucifixes they left along the shore of the river, the first environmental concept art on the North American continent.

In 1821, Mexico won its war of independence from Spain and took possession of the land. Then, in the summer of 1847, as U.S. troops were closing in on Mexico City, one hundred and seventy Mormon pioneers were moving west in covered wagons across the Great Plains toward the Great Basin. Both parties were moving under orders from God to take the land from Mexico. The government of the United States justified the war by saying it was our Manifest Destiny, the will of God, to extend the boundaries of freedom and democracy from coast to coast. The Mormons were looking for the place God had given them to build His Kingdom on Earth.

The Mormons got here first, arriving in the Salt Lake Valley in July 1847. The U.S. troops took Mexico City a few months later, in September. In March 1848, Mexico signed the Treaty of Guadalupe Hidalgo, selling, for $15 million, what is now California, Nevada, Utah, Arizona, and parts of New Mexico, Colorado, and Wyoming.

In April this year I made an offer on this house of close to a quarter of a million dollars, and it was accepted. Then I got a fair estimate on what the loan would cost and what the payments would be and I realized I was going to have a hard time making the payments and eating every month unless I had a partner helping me.

I brought Lisa to the house one last time and laid it on the line. I said, "Look, this is a good house. It's old, but it has good bones and good energy, lots of light and a great view of the mountains. We can live here until we die, but you'll need to get a job."

She said she felt like I was giving her an ultimatum. I said she was right, that I was forcing her to make a decision for her own good. I said, "It's not going to work, we're not going to work, unless you make a commitment." She said she wasn't ready and needed to be free to do other things. She felt that she had a mission in life and needed to pursue it. She also said she'd just found out she might have to go to Vietnam for a couple of months to work on her Agent Orange video with a Dutchman named Jan.

I said, "Jan?"

"My friend. You met him in Thailand. We had dinner, and you thought he was a loser."

"You're making a mistake," I said. "Don't do this to me; don't do this to us."

I bought the house and moved in by myself. Lisa stayed in the apartment we'd been renting. She was happy I got the house. She just didn't want to live with me, and this hurt, pretty bad, so I broke off the relationship in an email. I thought this would force her to come to reality, my reality, which was all about the future and it was going to be bad and then it was going to get worse.

When the pioneers arrived in 1847 there were no Native Americans living in the Salt Lake Valley. There were Shoshones along the Weber River thirty miles to the north, and Utes next to Utah Lake fifty miles to the south. These two tribes did not always get along, sometimes fighting and killing each other, so the land in between—the Salt Lake

Valley—was a no-man's-land, a buffer zone. The Mormons knew this, and this is why they settled here.

Under the leadership of their new prophet, Brigham Young, the Mormons quickly set out building the "State of Deseret," a mythic word taken from the Book of Mormon meaning "land of the honeybee." Within two years, they'd formed a civil government with a constitution, a representative legislature, a court system, a police force, and a standing militia to protect them from threats, which they foresaw would come from the Indians or the U.S. military, or both.

Within three years, Brigham Young had sent thousands of colonists to the far corners of the Great Basin and the Colorado Plateau. When he drew the border of his new state, in clockwise fashion, it ran from the Wind River mountains in Wyoming to the Rocky Mountains in Colorado, to the Gila Mountains in southern Arizona, to the Pacific Ocean at San Diego, and up the crest of the Sierras in California and then back to the Wind River—a circle with the temple in Salt Lake City at its center. Then gold was discovered at Sutter's Mill in Northern California, and the road to riches ran straight through the land of the honeybee.

The Mormons wanted to be admitted to the Union as a religious state. Their constitution was based upon the Law of God, the God of their prophet Joseph Smith and his holy book, the Book of Mormon. Many in Washington called for war, arguing it would be better to wipe out them out as soon as possible, before they grew any more numerous. But in 1849, instead of sending an army, President James K. Polk sent an expedition of the Corps of Topographical Engineers to survey the area surrounding the Great Salt

Lake. It was a mission of peace, and Lieutenant John Gunnison was second in charge under Captain Howard Stansbury.

As the party drew close to the valley, Stansbury was warned the Mormons would not receive them with kindness:

> Before reaching Great Salt Lake City, I had heard from various sources that much uneasiness was felt by the Mormon community at my anticipated coming among them. I was told that they would never permit any survey of their country to be made; while it was darkly hinted that if I persevered in attempting to carry it on, my life would scarce be safe.
>
> (Howard Stansbury, *Exploration and Survey of the Valley of the Great Salt Lake of Utah,* 1853, p. 84)

Stansbury decided to split the party into two groups that would enter the Salt Lake Valley from opposite directions. He led one group along the northern route, and Gunnison took a group of approximately eighteen men along the southern route, arriving in the Salt Lake Valley in late August, three days before Captain Stansbury.

In late August the sky would have been without a cloud— hot, dry air standing still as a bone. The treeless valley, twelve miles wide and twenty miles long, was dotted with adobe homes and small farms with cows, horses, pigs, and chickens. Riding through, the lieutenant asked the residents where he might find their leader, Brigham Young. Their response was silence. No one would talk to him. The party rode through town and camped on the north end of the valley, and that night, around the campfire, they were visited by the leader of

Brigham's secret police, the Sons of Dan, who told Gunnison that no one would be leaving the valley with any maps.

The next day Gunnison and Brigham Young faced off in the middle of a street near Temple Square, the heart of the city and the ontological foundation of the Mormon world. On one side there was Young, the man of faith, built like an aging linebacker, thick arms and hands made for crushing things, a mason by trade, with little formal education. On the other side there was Gunnison, a man of reason, second in his class at West Point, a charmer of women who could quote Virgil and Cicero in Latin.

Young snarled and told Gunnison, "I know why you're here. You're here to survey this valley into townships and sections and thereby take title to it. But that's not going to happen. This land is promised to us by God, and we have suffered greatly for it."

Gunnison said to Brigham, "Sir, I've heard how you and your people have been persecuted in the past, but let me assure you our mission is purely scientific. We're here to map the terrain and study its geologic features and biological species. We have an artist to make sketches. I draw some myself."

Young gritted his teeth and clenched his fists. He was no fool. He was the prophet, seer, and revelator of God's chosen people. He was king. For two years he'd had complete control, total authority over his people, and now his reign was being challenged by a dilettante. He was mad beyond words.

Gunnison said, "But surely Captain Stansbury will be here soon and he can explain everything to you."

Brigham walked away in a huff, and that was the end of the meeting.

When Stansbury showed up two days later, the three met and came to an agreement. The officers told Young they were very impressed with what he'd been able to accomplish—making the desert bloom, keeping the savages at bay—and they promised to support his appointment as territorial governor. As this was what Young really wanted and needed, he agreed to let the expedition continue and promised them food and supplies at a fair price.

Even though I'd told Lisa I wanted to split up, I was still trying to talk to her and make it work somehow. I think she was trying as well, until all of a sudden she wasn't. She told me she'd met "a friend" and they'd gone to a bar to hear some music. He liked music and dancing; she liked music and dancing; he was just "a friend." Then I found out she'd been seeing him a lot more, spending six nights a week with him. When I asked her about it, she said she needed to have fun and not feel so bad about herself.

She said I was too dark, too morose, and that I was smothering her. She broke down and sobbed and said she'd failed in making our relationship work and now she needed to have her own life and her own friends and figure out who she was and what she was going to do with her life. She said I needed to give her some space, some time, to figure things out.

I went back to my empty house. She was right. I'd been crushing her into the ground trying to get her to grow roots, and it just made her want to get away.

The Stansbury expedition began its topographic and scientific survey of the Salt Lake Valley and its environs. Before winter set in, they'd traveled the sterile circumference of the

Great Salt Lake, then headed for Utah Lake, fifty miles to the south, the land of the Ute Indians.

Although the men of science were able to communicate and compromise with the people of faith, they were definitely not up to this with the Indians. They didn't even try. They saw the Utes and all other native people as subhuman, an animal species, disgusting. This is Stansbury's description of their encounters with the natives during the fall of 1849:

> While engaged in the survey of the Utah Valley, we were no little annoyed by numbers of the [Utes], who hung around the camp, crowding around the cook-fires, more like hungry dogs than human beings, eagerly watching for the least scrap that might be thrown away, which they devoured with avidity and without the least preparation.
>
> (Stansbury, *Exploration and Survey*, p. 148)

When the Mormons first arrived in the Salt Lake Valley, they'd promised the Utes they wouldn't settle in their territory, to the south in Utah Valley. This promise lasted about eighteen months. By the spring of 1849, thirty Mormon families had settled along the Provo River, which feeds into Utah Lake. They built a fortress, grazed their cattle on the open range, and started taking as many as six thousand fish a day from the river to send to Salt Lake. The Utes responded by stealing some Mormon horses and shooting some cows.

The first battle between the Mormons and the Utes happened in March 1849. The Mormon militia surrounded a Ute camp and started shooting, killing four to seven men and wounding some women and kids, trying to punish them so badly they'd be afraid to ever again steal a horse or shoot a cow. A few months later, one of the Ute chiefs named Old Bishop was shot in cold blood by a Mormon settler. The body was disemboweled and filled with rocks and sunk in the river, where it was found a few days later by Old Bishop's family.

That winter, the winter of 1850, measles struck the Utes and they began to die. Desperate, they killed more Mormon cows for food. In February, while Stansbury's party was wintering over in Salt Lake City, Brigham Young asked Stansbury for advice on how to deal with the Utes. Should he attack or leave them alone? Stansbury told Young to attack, and John Gunnison agreed with him.

> [As] the forbearance already shown had been only attributed to weakness and cowardice, and had served but to encourage further and bolder outrages, I did not hesitate to say to them that, in my judgment, the contemplated expedition against these savage marauders was a measure not only of good policy, but one of absolute necessity and self-preservation.
>
> (Stansbury, *Exploration and Survey*, p. 149)

So on a cold February morning a force of one hundred Mormon militia surrounded a Ute camp along the Provo River and opened fire with rifles and a cannon filled with shrapnel. The killing took three days, as many of the Utes fled the scene and had to be tracked down in the snow. Somewhere between forty and seventy men were killed and as many women and children were taken as prisoners.

One of Brigham's secret police, or assassins, Bill Hickman, cut off the head of a Ute warrior named Big Elk and hung it from his porch inside the Mormon fort. The doctor with the Stansbury expedition happened to see the head hanging there and asked a couple of the Mormon militiamen if they could get him some more to send back to Washington so they could be measured and studied. The militiamen said, "Sure, there are plenty of bodies out there frozen in the snow and ice. We can get you some." Abner Blackburn was one of the men chosen to help the doctor in the name of science:

> A few days after the last battle with the Indians a
> government surgeon wanted James Or and me to take
> a sley cross over on the ice and secure the Indians
> heads for he wanted to send them to Washington to
> a medical institution. Hired a sley crost over the ice
> the weather was bitter cold. The surgeon took out
> his box of instruments and commenced it took him
> a quarter of an hour to cut of one head. The sun was
> getting low and freezing cold Jim and me took the
> job in our own hands we wear not going to wait on
> the surgeons slow motion jerked our knives out and
> had them all off in a few minutes they wear frozen
> and come of easy in our fassion the surgeon stood
> back and watched us finish the job the surgeon shot
> some ducks ten or twelve boxed them up guts feath-
> ers and all. And tole me to bring them down with the
> Indian heads in a week or two to Salt Lake City. Took
> them down according to agreement the weather
> turned warm and the ducks 14 wear green with rot.
> The Indian heads smelt loud drove to his office. And

told him the ducks wear spoilt he opened the box pulled out a wing smelt it and says they are just right. He settled up and invited me to super.

(Brigham D. Madsen,
Exploring the Great Salt Lake, 1989, p. 261)

I was lying in bed in my new house. I'd spent the afternoon building the bed, and now I was lying in it, thinking about Lisa being happy with her new friend and not me. I got up, put on my clothes, and drove down to her apartment. I walked in without knocking. It was 11:30 and she was in the bathtub. I told her to get out; we needed to talk. Then I grabbed her cell phone and threw it against the wall, stomped it into little pieces, tore the pieces into bits with my bare hands. I'd always hated that phone because it connected her to friends all over the world, places she lived before and might live again, good friends she still liked to visit. The phone, in my mind, was what kept her from being grounded. It was what kept her from doing what I knew was right.

And I didn't stop with breaking the phone. I told her I knew she'd been lying to me. I demanded the truth, but I didn't believe anything she told me. I got so mad I threatened to throw a flower vase through a window and then I threatened to throw it at her. Then I said I felt like choking her. I said it. I'd never said anything like that before, not to someone I loved. I should have been shot like a rabid dog. It was horrible. I was horrible.

In the fall of 1850, Stansbury completed his survey and returned to Washington, D.C., to write his report. Gunnison ended up writing his own book, *The Mormons or Latter-Day Saints*. Both

Scott Carrier

books sold well, but Gunnison's went through seven editions in the next five years, mainly because it had more information about Mormon culture and the lives of the polygamists.

Gunnison's book has three parts. The first is like an ethnography, describing Mormon beliefs and history from their point of view. They were hardworking, happy people, prone to dancing and spiritual ecstasies:

> —men and women falling to the floor in the public assemblies, wallowing, rolling, and tossing of hands—pointing into the heavens at "the cloud of witnesses"—uttering Indian dialects, and declaring that they would immediately convert them—there was swooning—rushing out of doors and running into the fields, some would mount stones and stumps, and speak in loud "tongues," some would pick up the stones and read from characters of writing, which were miraculously made, and then suddenly disappeared—others found pieces of parchment falling upon them, which they declared were sealed with the seal of Christ, and which they no sooner copied than they vanished.
>
> (Gunnison, *The Mormons*, 1852, p. 102)

The second part of the book relates the origin and history of the Mormon Church according to Gunnison's own investigation. In this part he paints an unflattering portrait of the Mormon prophet, Joseph Smith, saying his family was considered by neighbors to be destitute of moral character and that Smith himself was a con man who plagiarized the Book of Mormon from an unpublished romance novel called "Manuscript Found."

And we came to the melancholy conclusion that nothing is too absurd when it assures the name of religion, to have its thousands of votaries.

(Gunnison, The Mormons, p. 88)

In the last section of the book Gunnison makes his own recommendation as to how to respond to the Mormon threat. He says, "leave them alone, as persecution will only make them stronger." Gunnison's theory was that every time the Mormons had been persecuted, they grew greater in number and stronger in their faith. He recognized a new kind of enemy—one that feeds on being attacked, as in the story of the sorcerer's apprentice. This enemy was not physical; it could not be shot dead or blown apart or burned down or chopped to pieces. The enemy was a belief system, and it had tremendous power. Brigham Young, speaking at the opening of the Salt Lake Tabernacle in 1852, said:

> The kingdom will continue to increase, to grow, to spread and prosper more and more. Every time its enemies undertake to overthrow it, it will become more extensive and powerful; instead of its decreasing, it will spread the more, become more wonderful and conspicuous to the nations until it fills the whole earth.

(Discourse by President Brigham Young,
Delivered at the Opening of the New
Tabernacle, Great Salt Lake City, April 6, 1852,
Journal of Discourses, vol. 1, 1854–1886, p. 203)

Gunnison's solution was to leave them alone and let them tear themselves apart. He believed Joseph Smith and Brigham Young were false prophets and the Mormon people would eventually figure this out.

> The causes which are at work to break up the clanship and the oneness of the Mormon State, are among themselves. The bursting power is internal, and loosening the outward bands will discover it . . . If let alone . . . they well learn how and when to throw off the usurpations of a pretended Theocracy.
>
> (Gunnison, *The Mormons*, p. 157)

Gunnison's book came out in 1852, and in 1853 he was promoted to captain and recommissioned by the Corps of Topographical Engineers to scout a possible route for the transcontinental railroad through southern Colorado and central Utah. He wrote to Brigham Young, telling him he would be passing through the territory and would perhaps winter over again in Salt Lake. He received no reply. When his expedition reached the Utah Territory in the late fall, the settlers greeted him as if they hadn't known he was coming.

He was about one hundred and fifty miles south of Salt Lake City, close to the new territorial capital of Fillmore. The Mormons in Fillmore told him there had been some fighting with the Indians, and that recently an Indian had been killed by some emigrants on their way to California, but they assured him everything was calm and peaceful at the moment.

Two days later, in the early morning as Gunnison and his men were waking up in their camp, they were attacked by a band of Ute Indians, or men dressed as Ute Indians, or both. Of the eleven men who were with Gunnison, seven were killed and four got away on their horses. Gunnison was shot while pleading with his attackers.

"Stop," he cried, "we're your friends."

His still-beating heart was cut from his body, then his arms were cut off below the elbows. Some of his men were decapitated. The bodies were left on the ground to be devoured by wolves.

The survivors agreed the party had been attacked by Indians, but the word on the streets in Salt Lake was the Sons of Dan, Brigham Young's secret police, disguised as Indians, had staged the killings as revenge for what Gunnison had written in his book.

To this day no one really knows what happened, although some historians believe the Gunnison massacre was a test run for the massacre at Mountain Meadows in 1857, in which Sons of Dan dressed as Indians slaughtered one hundred and twenty men, women, and children passing through Utah on their way to California.

It's also possible that Gunnison and his men were killed as revenge for the 1850 massacre of Utes along the Provo River near Fort Utah. We'll never know for sure, and somehow I don't even care anymore. What I care about is Gunnison's proposal—that the Mormons should be left alone.

The morning after I freaked out and become violent, I somehow convinced Lisa to drive out in the desert with me, where we could talk without being crazy. We drove west on the old Pony Express trail, a dirt road, to a valley south of the Dugway Proving Grounds, where the U.S.

government tests agents of biological and chemical warfare. It was a beautiful day, a big sky with different kinds of clouds coming from the north over the Great Salt Lake. We watched their shadows race across the grass and sagebrush ten miles away. I was calmed down; she was calmed down.

"It's so beautiful out here," she said. "Why can't we live here?"

"How would we make money?" I asked.

"Pretty soon there isn't going to be any money," she said. "You're right about everything changing, and maybe things are going to get really bad, but you can't control it. And you can't control me either. You've got to lighten up. You may own a house, but you don't own me."

I told her everything I could think of—how I'd been wrong, how I treated her very badly, how we could fix everything and still make it work, how I loved her and couldn't imagine living without her. That I freaked out because I was scared she was leaving me.

She said, "Everything you do now, you do because you're scared. You bought the house because you're scared, you tell me to get a job because you're scared, you threaten to kill me because you're scared, but you're just scared of yourself, and these are all projections of your own mind. Everything you do, it only makes things worse, and I can't take it anymore. I have to leave."

It wasn't until we were back in town and I'd dropped her off for probably the last time that I realized I was doing the same thing as the sorcerer's apprentice. He created a slave using magic he didn't really understand, and when the slave got out of control he tried to kill it. He acted out of fear. I acted out of fear. The Mormons acted out of fear with the Indians. The United States acted out of fear with the terrorists.

Acting out of fear only makes the problem worse. This is the answer, the source of the spell, the place from which it arises. A sorcerer understands the origins of things, and this is how he gains power over them.

Gunnison was saying, *Don't act out of fear. Don't be afraid of the Mormons.* He believed the American genius was the spirit of liberty and human freedom and it was stronger than fear. Abraham Lincoln said:

> Our reliance is in the love of liberty which God has planted in us. Our defense is in the spirit which prizes liberty as the heritage of all men, in all lands everywhere. Destroy this spirit and you have planted the seeds of despotism at your own doors. Familiarize yourselves with the chains of bondage and you prepare your own limbs to wear them. Accustomed to trample on the rights of others, you have lost the genius of your own independence and become the fit subjects of the first cunning tyrant who rises among you.
>
> (Abraham Lincoln's speech at Edwardsville,
> Illinois, September 11, 1858, quoted in
> *Lincoln on Democracy*, edited by Mario M.
> Cuomo and Harold Holzer, 2004, p. 128)

So, I ask you, what would happen if we left the terrorists alone? What if we pull our troops from their holy land and let them live like in the days of Mohammed? Why can't we be brave enough to let them test *sharia* against the love of liberty? Would the harm be greater than what comes from violence, from responding out of fear? I think it would be far less. It's not that we do nothing, but that we do nothing out of fear. If we're not afraid of terrorists, then they lose.

Lisa has gone, left town, to work on a ranch in southern Utah. She wrote me an email saying she loves it but doesn't know if she's going to stay. She doesn't know where she'll end up or what she should be doing. I'm trying to leave her alone, let her figure things out for herself. I shaved my head. I need to lighten up. I need to work on this house and try not to act out of fear anymore.

Najibullah in America

Orem, Utah, 2011

I first met Najibullah Niazi in Afghanistan in the late fall of 2001, at the beginning of the longest war in American history. I'd just arrived in the country and was walking around the city of Mazar-i-Sharif, which had been recently evacuated by the Taliban. In the center of the city, next to the mosque, I was suddenly surrounded by fifty to a hundred men and boys and they were all yelling at me. They knew I was an American and they wanted answers. I tried to show them with body language that I did not speak their language and therefore did not know what they were saying, but this had little to no effect upon them. I sat down on a park bench, thinking they'd grow tired and walk away. They only drew in closer, tighter, their voices spinning me up in a cocoon, and I thought, "Oh, man, they got me."

Suddenly there was a person who looked like Sinead O'Connor sitting next to me—a shaved head, big green eyes with long eyelashes, a Hard Rock Café T-shirt under an old ski parka, polyester bell-bottom pants. Maybe a boy, maybe a girl, a voice so calm.

"Sir, I am wondering if you need some help."

"What are they saying?" I asked.

"They are saying many things but basically only one thing: 'How long before America brings money and food?'"

"I have no idea," I said.

"Yes, they know this already, but they want to ask."

"Can you make them go away?" I asked. And with this the angel-like being stood up and yelled at the crowd, something short but very sharp, and they all shut up and left.

"What did you say?" I asked.

"I told them this was not the Afghan way to treat a guest and they all should be ashamed for their families."

Meeting Najib was like meeting a ball of energy that mysteriously appeared and saved my ass. It took me a few minutes to figure out he was a human being, a boy. For the next three weeks, until I left the country, he was my guide and translator, the best I ever had. He could go anywhere and talk to anybody with charm and cunning. He could shape-shift, and he could lie—never to hurt anybody but only to get by and survive.

He was only seventeen then. Now he's twenty-seven and graduating from the state university where I work as a professor—Utah Valley University in Orem, Utah. We're both wearing caps and gowns and flat-topped hats with tassels. He's sitting on the floor of the basketball arena with the graduating class, and I am up in the stands with the faculty and families. Every fourth person among the families is an infant, and many of them are crying. The man giving the commencement speech is a member of the local business community and he is continually breaking down and sobbing, struggling to hold himself upright at the podium. He's been saying things that would be appropriate at BYU or the semiannual Mormon Conference, but not at a state university.

> May you sanctify this great education by understanding that it is but a declaration that you are God's answer to the human dilemma, and in understanding that this is not an end but an invitation to go into this world . . . [unintelligible due to sobbing] . . . to hear His words and suffer His scars, and again you will become as you do so a builder of souls and not a passerby in the mainstream of mediocrity. God bless you, thank you very much.

This is where we ended up. UVU and the Mormons took us both in from the cold, but now Najib is getting out and I may be here to stay, at least for the time being.

Before I left Afghanistan in 2001, I asked Najib for his address.

"Address?" he asked.

"Where you get your mail," I said.

"Mail?" he asked.

"From the post office," I replied.

"Post office?"

He'd never heard of such a thing. Afghanistan had trucks and roads, but it had never had a government capable of delivering the mail in his lifetime. So we stayed in touch by phone. Najib found a job as an assistant to the radio operator at the United Nations office in Mazar, and he'd call me from work. Two or three times a year, my phone would ring at 3:00

to 4:00 AM and I'd hold it to my ear and fall into a cloud of static, cracklings of cosmic rays, and there would be Najib's thin, high voice whispering so his boss wouldn't hear.

"How is your family?" was always the first thing he'd say.

"My family is a mess," I'd say. "But everyone is healthy, so that's good."

Eventually we'd get around to talking about his safety. General Dostum's men were after him, he said, because of some things I'd written in the story about my trip to Afghanistan, published in *Harper's* in 2002. I'd said that Dostum was known in northern Afghanistan as a cold-blooded killer, and somehow, according to Najib, Dostum found out about it and had put Najib's name on his list of people to kill.

Najib said he'd been warned that Dostum's men were looking for him, and he needed to get out of the country. I believed he was in danger, but not from Dostum's men. They could have found him if they really wanted to. He was just in a genuinely dangerous place, a war zone, where he'd put himself at greater risk by working for foreigners who were seen by many Afghans to be infidels and invaders. He could have easily been killed as a way of sending a message, a warning, to others.

I tried to think of a way to get him out, but I didn't know how to do it until 2006, after I'd been talking to some professors at UVU who were trying to get me to take a job in the Department of Communication. One of these professors, Scott Abbott, had some clout within the administration. I thought maybe he could pull some strings to get Najib accepted as a student. I knew Najib had dropped out of school when he was twelve to go to work on the streets to make some money for his family, and it might be quite a jump for him to go straight into college in the United States, but I also knew he could do it. I told him to write a letter addressed to Dr. Scott Abbott.

"What do I say in the letter?" he asked.

"Write about your work experience," I said. "Describe the jobs you had when you quit school to make money for your family. When you're done, send it to me by email and I'll make suggestions and corrections and send it back to you. Then you can write it again, and we'll do this three or four times until it's ready to send."

I figured if he could show competency in writing then I could argue, or suggest, that he didn't need a high school diploma. And yet I knew he'd learned English from watching American movies—*Rush Hour* and *Rambo*—and probably didn't have much experience reading and writing the language, so I expected that it would take a while to get him up to speed. But I knew he could do it because writing is mainly about the movement of the mind, and Najib's mind moved like a Ferrari.

Three weeks later I got the first draft by email. It was barely readable—full of misspellings, grammatical and syntactical errors, problems with punctuation and capitalization, and so on. Still, once you figured out what he was saying, it was an amazing story.

He began with the Russians pulling out of Afghanistan in 1989, when he was five years old. There was peace for a few years, but there were no jobs or money, just a lot of weapons and ammunition left over from the war, so the only thing people could do when they got hungry was go kill somebody and take whatever they had, and this is how the Afghan civil war started. For six years, from 1992 to 1998, the various ethnic groups—Pashtuns, Uzbeks, Tajiks, and Hazaras—all fought each other for ultimate control of the country.

During this time Najib was in grade school on the outskirts of Mazar-i-Sharif. He admitted that he was a bad student, often falling asleep in class or skipping school to go into town and work collecting fares on buses making 10 cents a day. Najib's family had no money and was living on his uncle's farm. His father had been a geology professor at Balkh University, but the school closed down when the Russians left, so he was out of work and in hiding—from people who saw him as a Soviet sympathizer. When Najib was twelve years old, he asked his father if he could quit school and go to work every day to make some more money. At first his father said no, telling him that no matter how much money he could make now, he'd be able to make ten times that much later if he stayed in school. But Najib kept asking and finally his father agreed. He'd keep Najib's two older brothers in school because this would be better for the family in the long run, but in order to get by in the present he was willing to sacrifice Najib's future.

At first Najib made money by buying gasoline in the city, filling one-liter bottles and carrying them ten miles out of the city to sell for a few cents' profit per liter. Then he built a vendor box, like the kind used to carry hot dogs at baseball games, but he filled it with gum and cigarettes. He made as much as a dollar a day hawking his wares on the street.

At that time, in 1996, the largely Pashtun Taliban had taken control of all Afghanistan except for the area around Mazar-i-Sharif, where General Abdul Rashid Dostum and his Uzbek militia were in charge. Najib was afraid of Dostum's men even then, as they sometimes abducted young boys and forced them to dance and then raped them. He went to work every day afraid he wouldn't come home. Najib believed the Taliban had higher morals than Dostum's men and so he wanted them to come to Mazar and take over. Which they did, or tried to do, in 1997.

The word on the street was the Taliban were on their way from Herat to Mazar and would arrive in hours or days. Najib was selling gum and cigarettes when he saw the first tank come racing into the city at full speed, flying a dirty white cotton flag and carrying men with long beards, "southern style." Everybody started screaming, "It's the Taliban!" and ran away.

Najib ran ten miles to his home and got there just as the shooting started in the city. The battle went on for three days, and in the end Dostum's militia killed every single Talib, five thousand in all, and left their bodies in the streets. A couple of days after the shooting stopped, Najib went back into the city and saw the bodies still lying in the street, being eaten by wild dogs. The smell of death was everywhere.

A year later, in August 1998, the Taliban mounted a second assault, and this time they took the city, expelling the Uzbek militia and sending Dostum into exile. Because the Taliban were Pashtun, they could not "forgive their blood" and proceeded to go door-to-door in Mazar, looking for anyone with Uzbek (Mongolian) or Hazara (Persian) facial features and then pulling them into the street and shooting them in front of their homes. This time there were eight to nine thousand bodies for the wild dogs to feed upon.

The Taliban imposed sharia and inflicted its harsh punishments. Najib would walk around the city, passing the bodies of men hanging from lampposts, their mouths stuffed with money. He watched public executions of women who had shamed their families. At night, in his friend's basement, he watched smuggled videos from America and dreamed of someday being able to go there.

It was a mind-blowing essay, written in a form in which even the words seemed to have been blown apart. My original plan was to make corrections and send it back to Najib, but I decided to send it to Scott Abbott without changing a thing. He wrote back in less than an hour, saying, "We want him. Tell him he's accepted."

Four months later Najib was at my apartment in Salt Lake City. Two weeks after that he found a roommate with an apartment across the street from the UVU campus in Orem, safe in the warm bosom of Mormonia.

Scott Abbott was one of the professors who talked me into taking the job at UVU. He was a Mormon with a Ph.D. from Princeton who'd been a tenured professor at BYU but had left out of disgust with the administration and moved five miles northwest to UVU, then Utah Valley State College. UVSC had started in 1941 as a vocational school, grew into a two-year college, and then began granting four-year degrees in 1993. Scott and a few other BYU-escapee professors redesigned the curriculum, inserting a mandatory course in values and ethics as a way of trying to open the students' minds to cultures and traditions other than their own. They also tried to recruit professors from the liberal fringe of Mormonism, hiring a friend of mine, poet Alex Caldiero. Then they hired Phil Gordon, a rabble-rousing Jew from Chicago who became the chairman of the communications department. These three—Scott, Alex, and Phil—then came after me.

They told me I'd have complete academic freedom, that no one would tell me what to teach or how to teach, but that I'd have to justify my methods in terms of pedagogical theory or something like it that we could make up later. Phil said he'd help me with that part. Phil would be my boss and he would help me with everything and he promised me that it wasn't so bad that all, or almost all, the students were Mormons. He said he had, in fact, learned to become a better teacher and scholar because of it.

I didn't want to take the job because I thought it would mean admitting I'd failed as an independent writer and radio producer, and I didn't feel that I'd failed. I'd been turning out stories on a regular schedule, more than ever, for the NPR program *Hearing Voices*. In June 2006, I picked up a Peabody Award in New York City for a show we produced on illegal immigration. Most of our money, however, came from the Corporation for Public Broadcasting, and in 2006 the CPB cut most of its funding for independent radio producers.

I was heavily in debt, having always spent more money on stories than I made and covering the payments by taking out equity loans on our home. My friends and family, who were aware of my financial situation, were all telling me that if I didn't take the job I'd be acting very irresponsibly. I remember my first day of work, driving fifty miles south on the freeway during rush hour, thinking my life was over and from now on I was going to die very slowly.

I took the job and I hated it and the result was that I was a lousy teacher. The first comment posted about me on rate yourprofessor.com was, "Horrible! Horrible! Horrible!" and it just got worse from there.

Najib was not one of my students because he was an economics major in the school of business and I taught journalism courses and an introduction to mass communication. My students were mostly public relations majors who only took my classes because they were required. I didn't like these students—first because they were public relations majors and second because they were Mormons.

I grew up among Mormons, I live among Mormons, my best friends come from Mormon families . . . I do not hate the Mormons. But to live among them and see them in the grocery store or in their cars is one thing, whereas being surrounded by Mormons in a classroom is something else altogether. It's suffocating.

As I spoke in class, it felt like I was trapped in a large block of Jell-O. I could speak, but it was hard to breathe. I could speak and my students could hear me, but my words had different meanings for them, so no real communication ever happened. They just sat there and looked at me wondering what I did to get put inside a big block of Jell-O.

On the first day of my first journalism class I told the students there were only three rules in journalism and I could explain them in ten minutes. The rest was practice.

"The first rule," I said, "is tell the truth, or at least try to tell the truth. I'm fifty years old, and I still don't know what the truth is or how to tell it. So I try, and accept the consequences."

I saw their faces tighten and their eyes squint to focus, as if they were thinking, *Who is this guy?*

They already knew the truth and how to tell it because this was part of their religion. For them, the truth was a list called the Articles of Faith, and they all had it memorized.

For them, the truth was a matter of faith. For me, the truth was a matter of reason and logic. Same word, different meaning.

Moving on, I said, "The second rule of journalism is that the journalist must serve as an independent monitor of power." Then I quoted Edward Abbey:

> The moral duty of the free writer is to begin his work at home: to be a critic of his own community, his own country, his own government, his own culture . . . I believe that words count, that writing matters, that poems, essays, and novels—in the long run—make a difference. If they do not, then in the words of my exemplar Aleksandr Solzhenitsyn, the writer's work is of no more importance than the barking of village dogs at night.
>
> (Abbey, "A Writer's Credo," in *One Life at a Time, Please*, 1988, pp. 161–162)

The students could understand the idea of questioning authority. After all, it's a common theme of Hollywood movies—the good little guy stands up to the big bad guy and takes him down—but as for actually doing it themselves, no, it wasn't going to happen, especially not on a local level. They lived in a culture of obedience. Obedience was their first principle of heaven and their twelfth article of faith: "We believe in being subject to kings, presidents, rulers, and magistrates, in obeying, honoring, and sustaining the law."

There's a saying that all Mormons know—"When the prophet speaks, the thinking has been done." The prophet speaks and his words carry down through the church hierarchy step-by-step to the common member who obeys as proof of his or her faith, a mighty pyramid of obeisance. So my asking my students to question authority was, to them, no different than asking that they go against their religion, and they just weren't going to do it.

"The third rule of journalism," I said, "is that the journalist works for the public, not the publisher. Normally, when you have a job you owe your loyalty to the person who signs your paychecks, but a journalist owes his loyalty to the people who read or watch or listen to his stories. This means that good journalists often get fired and end up unemployable because they won't take orders from their bosses and have to make it on their own as freelancers or independents, with no regular paychecks or health insurance, living alone in low-rent apartments where they die from drinking and smoking too much."

I pretty much lost that class in less than an hour, and the rest of the semester was a nightmare.

Also that semester, in a different class, I succeeded in emptying the room—every student got up and walked out. It happened in my Introduction to Mass Communication class. I was showing a video of the 1972 Vietnam War documentary *Hearts and Minds*. In my introduction I explained how the film strengthened the antiwar movement and helped change the course of history. It was an example of a story that made a difference.

Everything was fine through the first half of the movie. Nobody seemed to mind the images of bombs dropping on villages or of the resulting civilian carnage, but then there was a scene in which two U.S. soldiers were in two beds with two Vietnamese prostitutes. The prostitutes were naked and the soldiers' hands were upon their breasts. The students saw it as pornography, and they were constantly being told by their church leaders not to watch pornography.

The exodus began with four students, both boys and girls, who packed their bags and got up from their seats. Then the whole class of about thirty followed them out of the room. I sat there watching the movie by myself, fuming mad. I'd bet my house that every student in that room had watched R-rated movies and had seen naked breasts before and liked it, but they couldn't do it as a group—when others were watching them, when they were all watching each other watching the naked breasts together. This was so scary it made them all run away.

This is why I didn't like my students and why, in return, they did not like me.

Najib, however, got along with the young Mormons quite well. He made friends easily, especially friends who were girls. Imagine a young Johnny Depp playing an exuberant Afghan refugee and you pretty much have Najibullah in America. He'd bat his long eyelashes a couple of times and smile and women of all ages would go weak in the knees. It was ridiculous. In Afghanistan the only women he knew were his mother and his sisters, but in America he was a rock star—changing his look from day to day, sometimes a goatee, sometimes a ponytail.

The Utah Valley is home to both Utah Valley University, with thirty thousand students, and Brigham Young University, with twenty thousand students. Anywhere else in the country, this many students packed into a relatively small area would produce a huge party scene, but the Mormon Church long ago figured out how to stop this from ever happening. Most of the students who go to either school end up living in privately owned, off-campus apartment complexes that enforce what is known as the BYU Living Standard, which means that every occupant signs a contract promising not to have alcohol in their apartments and not to entertain guests of the opposite sex after 10:00 PM on weekdays and 1:00 AM on weekends.

It's not a law; it's more a community agreement, and it works because the apartment complexes function like prisons where the students all watch each other to make sure no rules are broken. If someone drinks a beer or has a friend in a room after curfew then they're reported, often by their friends, and they get kicked out of their apartments. You'd think they wouldn't rat each other out, but they do, very quickly and easily, because they believe God is watching them and so they must.

I would never have been able to live in a place like that, but Najib had no problem. Compared to the Taliban, the Mormons were a cakewalk.

The only real problem he had with the Mormons, or the good Mormons, was that they were always trying to convert him, which for Najib was like someone trying to smother him. He tried to tell them conversion was not possible for a Pashtun. A Pashtun who becomes a Christian is no longer a Pashtun. He is either banished or killed. But the good Mormons just didn't get it.

So he fell in with a small gang of "bad Mormons" on campus who never tried to convert him. These so-called bad Mormons had, for various reasons, lost their faith and fallen away from the church, and like most people their age they were into sex and drugs and rock and roll. They lived in old rented houses or at home with their parents. They liked to party, and so did Najib, only he didn't indulge in the vices, being a Muslim, which made him a good designated driver.

I didn't offer very much advice to Najib on his education. He seemed set on studying business, and that just was not my domain. I did, however, make him take a couple of classes. The first was a course on Dada taught by my friend Alex Caldiero, the father of Momo, a kind of Mormon Dada.

Alex is a philosopher and a poet from the ancient tradition of mind-blowing non-sense. He was born in Sicily and moved to New York City with his family when he was nine. When he was in his late twenties he had a mystical experience in his apartment in Brooklyn and afterward he converted to Mormonism and moved to Orem. He's more of an old-style Mormon, more into trances and speaking in tongues than priesthood meeting or family home evening. In 2008, he did an antiwar protest in an auditorium on campus in which he wore a white gas mask and beat on an empty mortar shell while a friend accompanied him on an electric guitar that sounded like a slow-motion crash of a jetliner. Someone pulled the plug and cut the lights.

Anyway, I told Najib to take Alex's Dada class and I'd help him write the paper he'd have to turn in for the final exam. When the time arrived for him to write the paper, I told him, "Let's go for a drive up into the mountains."

My plan was to teach him how to write the way he talks, or would like to talk. We drove up Provo Canyon, following the Provo River, past the turnoff to the Sundance Ski Resort, up to the Heber Valley, a place they call "Little Switzerland."

"Take out a pen and some paper and tell me, 'Who were the Dadaists?'" I said.

Najib put his notebook in his lap and sucked his pen and said, "The Dadaists were artists in Europe who thought art had too many rules and was boring, so they moved to Zurich in Switzerland where there were no rules about art."

"Excellent," I said. "Write that down, just what you said."

It took him about five minutes and when he read it back he'd completely changed the wording and it made no sense at all—exactly what my other students would do. They'd tell me a story and it would be fine, and I'd tell them to write down what they just said and then they'd mess it all up by trying to make it sound proper.

"Look down at the river," I said. "Do you see any places where you could jump from rock to rock and make it across to the other side?"

"No," he said, "there is too much water."

"Well, imagine there is a place like that. I want you to think about writing as jumping from rock to rock. Can you swim?"

"Not very well."

"Good. If you fall, you'll drown. In order to jump to a rock you must answer my question honestly in your own voice, not the voice of someone else. If you try to answer in someone else's voice, you'll fall into the river and drown. Do you understand?"

"Yes."

"You've jumped to the first rock by telling me who the Dadaists were. Now jump again and tell me, 'What did the Dadaists do?'"

"They sat in coffee shops and talked about new ways to make art."

"Did they come up with anything?"

"They said art should have no rules. Whatever was pleasing to them, they called it art."

"So what was pleasing to them?"

"The one called Duchamp took a toilet and turned it upside down to make people see it for its shape, not what it does."

"And what do you think about that?"

"But what I think doesn't matter," he said.

"So now you're in the middle of the stream and you're just going to stay there?" I asked. "Will I have to call your father and tell him you were last seen in the middle of a river contemplating Dada? In order to keep going you have to say what you think. Now, jump!"

"Back home we were given assignments and the teacher told us, 'This is what I want you to write,' and we just followed instructions. If we wrote what we thought, we would get beaten up by the teacher."

"Do you think Alex is going to beat you up?" I asked.

"No. He told us to write what we think. He said that's what he wants to know."

"Then go for it. What did you think about the upside-down toilet?"

"For me, it worked, because a toilet is a very dirty thing, the most dirty thing, but when I saw the picture of it I didn't see it as a toilet. I saw it as a beautiful shape. Duchamp was trying to show there is more than one way to see the same thing, and for me that blew my mind."

"Very good," I said, "write that down, everything you just said."

"Starting where?" he asked.

"Starting back at the beginning."

It took a while, during lunch in a café in Heber, to get everything down the way he said it, the way he put the pieces together.

On the way home I said, "You're still out in the river. You've got a couple more rocks before you get to the other side, and this next jump is the hardest one of all. You've told me who the Dadaists were, what they did, and what you think about it; now tell me if learning this stuff made any difference in your life or changed the way you see yourself and the world around you."

"For me, when Alex talked about the Dadaists, I thought he was talking about my friends here at school. The Dadaists liked to hang out and take drugs and go crazy and then they would sleep with each other. This is what my friends do, even though it is against the rules of their society. They used to believe in those rules, but now they don't. They want there to be no rules."

"And how does that make you feel?" I asked.

"How does it make me feel?" he asked.

"Yes, do you have feelings? Do you know what they are?"

I asked this as a joke, but when I said it I thought about Najib walking through a street filled with dead bodies and wondered if I was being too harsh.

"It is fun and scary at the same time," he said.

"Yes, good," I said, "and what's the word for that kind of feeling—fun and scary at the same time?"

He thought about it for a while, maybe five miles, and then said, "I don't know."

"This is the last rock," I said. "You make this one, you're

across the river to the other side. Think about it. What's the word to describe those feelings?"

He thought some more and couldn't come up with it, so I told him.

"Freedom," I said. "Fun and scary at the same time is called 'freedom,' and that's what America is all about."

I gave him the ending, just as many others have done for me in the past.

The Prophet Gordon B. Hinckley died on the day I was planning to lecture on Thomas Paine and his best-selling 1776 pamphlet, *Common Sense*. But then when I was driving to work I noticed that the American flags along the freeway were flying at half-mast. I turned on the radio and heard the news. President Hinckley, who was ninety-seven years old and had not been in good health, had passed away. It was a sad thing because everybody loved Gordon B. Hinckley—Mormons, non-Mormons, even I loved Gordon B. Hinckley. He was the Mormon Dalai Lama. But I thought Thomas Paine would turn over in his grave if he knew we were flying the flag at half-mast for a dead prophet.

Paine was a Deist who didn't believe in prophets. He believed God created the natural world and the universe and then He split, and He hasn't been seen or heard from since. *Common Sense* was an attack on monarchy, or the divine rule of a king. Paine's argument posed this basic question: If God sanctions the power of King George, why is he such a tyrant? Common sense tells us it's all a big lie and that there's a better form of government, one based on natural law—reason and science—rather than religion. The book broke all records for sales and inspired the American Revolution. Many of Paine's suggestions for the new form of government were included in the U.S. Constitution, such as the idea that the government should not make laws about religious beliefs.

I was going to argue that America was born from Paine's position that God is not present, that He's not watching us or speaking to anybody and He never has. I was going to tell them they didn't have to believe this, but they should at least understand that there's an origin myth of America other than the one they know, which goes like this: Jesus Christ created the United States of America by raising up our founding fathers and then guiding their hands in writing the Declaration of Independence and the Constitution. Once protections for religious freedom were in place, Jesus directed Joseph Smith to found an entirely new religion, restoring the true gospel, and begin building the Kingdom of God on Earth in preparation for His Second Coming.

I wanted to tell them how the meaning and power of a thing lies in its origin, and this is why origin myths are important. The way we understand ourselves and the world around us has a lot to do with the story we tell about where we came from. So someone who believes America was created by Jesus is going to have quite a different personal identity and worldview than someone who believes America was created by men who were trying to leave Jesus out of it. I wanted my students to at least think about this.

But when I got to class I realized my planned lecture wasn't going to work at all. The students came in and I told them I had prepared a lecture about Thomas Paine, one of our founding fathers, but, on account of the prophet dying, I was going to cancel the class.

"You can all go," I said.

They thought that was strange. None of their other professors were canceling class. They wanted to know more.

I shouldn't have said anything else. I should have just left. Instead, I said, "And I'm doing this out of respect for Paine, not for the prophet."

The students looked at me as if I could not have said anything more insulting, even though most of them didn't know who Thomas Paine was. Now they'll just associate him with a mean and stupid professor they had in college.

When Najib came to America, he wanted to be a part of my family. I knew he needed to be grounded this way, through a family, because in Afghanistan everything makes sense or has meaning through the family, and I didn't want him to feel alone, as if he were floating in outer space. Unfortunately, I was just barely a member of my own family, having been separated from my wife . . . and so on. I was something of an outcast, and I kind of let him down in this way. However, both Najib and I were invited to holiday dinners.

On Thanksgiving 2009 we were all sitting around the table, ten or twelve people, with two or three conversations going on at once, when suddenly there was only one person talking and it was Najib saying how most of my students hate me. This wasn't exactly breaking news to my family as I'd done nothing but complain about my job for two years, but I don't think I ever described the situation with the word "hate."

He'd been talking to my daughter, telling her how much he'd learned from his friends in Orem and how they are all bad Mormons and that they are all like me, but there were only about ten of them. The rest of the students, thirty thousand or so, were all good Mormons and they hated me. And at this point he had the ears and eyes of everyone in the room.

"I hear what they say about you behind your back," he said, looking at me.

"Like what?" I asked.

"Like you show pornography in class and insult their prophet."

"Oh, Scott!" my mother gasped.

"But this is because they are good Mormons and they have to think this way," Najib said. "They are the Mormon Taliban."

He explained how his friends in Orem used to be good Mormons but then they stopped believing in certain things, things they realized were not the word of God but the words of men who were trying to control other people. He was trying to say that he'd learned from hanging out with bad Mormons that some of his beliefs were tribal practices and not the rules of God.

"For instance," he said, "I would no longer tie my sister to a tree and shoot her with a Kalashnikov if she slept with a man who was not her husband."

Everyone at the table knew this story because I'd written about it. When I was in Afghanistan I'd asked Najib a theoretical question: What would happen if your sister slept with a man who was not her husband? Najib replied that his father would tie her to a tree and shoot her with a Kalashnikov. So I said, "What if he wouldn't do it?" And Najib said his oldest brother would do it, and if not him, then his next oldest brother, and if not him, then he, Najib, would do it.

"Najib," I said, "don't tell me you'd kill your own sister. I know it's your custom and everything, but think about it. You wouldn't actually do it."

This made him so mad that he quit. He went home that night thinking he wasn't coming back in the morning. Luckily, his dad talked him down. Najib told him he couldn't work for an infidel who insulted his family in this way. His dad asked him, "What exactly did he say? Did he actually say anything bad about our family, or was he just asking a hypothetical question? Maybe where he comes from, this is not a rude thing to do." So Najib came back the next day, but, he said, only because he'd given me his word that he would stay with me until I left Afghanistan, and that he would honor this Pashtun tradition.

This had always been in the back of my head, and sometimes I worried that something would really piss him off and he'd go jihadi on us. So when he announced that he'd no longer kill his sister I was greatly relieved.

A couple of weeks later I asked Najib to explain how the whole thing worked, how shooting your daughter or sister could be a sanctioned behavior in his culture, because I still didn't understand it. We sat in his car and talked for three hours, and when we were done I had a better idea of how it works.

People in Afghanistan live in a tribal culture. A tribe is basically a large gang of families, and when a decision has to be made—say how to allocate water or whether to go to war—each family sends a representative to the tribal council, where a debate takes place. The debate ends not with a vote, but with consensus, in which everybody agrees. So in order to get your way in a tribal council, you have to be able to persuade everybody to agree with you. But if your family has lost its honor, everybody is just going to laugh at you, and they will keep laughing at you until you go away, move with your family to another village, or kill someone—either the person who shamed your family or the person making the accusation.

Najib's basic point was that in a tribal culture nothing is more important than your family's honor, not even money.

"Everybody wants to be pure," he said. "Everyone wants to be part of an ideal family, just basically people of God, they are so clean of sin. When you asked about my sister the only thing I knew was that if my sister does something bad, our neighbors are going to laugh at us, and the only thing that will stop them laughing at us is to just get rid of her. The only thing she is worth is a bullet. Back then the only thing I knew was the tribal influence. Now I've learned more about myself, about humanity, and what it means to be a human, especially what it means to be a woman."

He told me how embarrassed he felt when he started taking classes and some of the girls would get better grades than he did, and then how surprised he was when he asked them how they did it and they offered to show him, to tutor him on their own time.

"Now I know that women are twice as smart as men," he said. "They have more faith, more loyalty, and they are cleaner than men."

"But would you marry an American girl?" I asked, knowing that he still thought a lot of American girls were no better than prostitutes.

"I would have married Leia," he said. Leia was his girlfriend for a couple of years. "But her mother didn't like that I have brown skin."

"And what would your family in Afghanistan have thought?"

"It would have been very bad for my family as well. If I want to get married, I either have to go back to Afghanistan or find a Pashtun girl who lives in America."

"Do you think that's possible?"

"In California there are many Afghan families," he said, "so maybe I will find someone there."

I didn't want to suck at my job. I didn't want to feel like a fraud and a failure; nobody does. So I tried to become a better teacher. I stopped criticizing the prophets—that helped. I also admitted that I had to give assignments and then grade them, with comments. I'd been practicing a pedagogy based on not giving assignments, as I truly dreaded reading the finished work, but my efforts only lent more support to the theory that students need to do exercises and then get feedback. Otherwise, they don't learn anything.

I found that quizzes worked well, as they forced the students to keep up on the reading and also come to class, which they didn't do if they didn't have to. Mainly, I just accepted that I wasn't going to be able to open their minds by force, as it only caused them to shut more firmly. Strangely, about this same time they started to change on their own, for reasons that had nothing to do with me.

In the fall of 2010, the beginning of my fourth year on campus, I was giving a news quiz in a journalism class—ten questions about current local, national, and international news. One of the questions was: "What New York City bridge did Tyler Clementi jump from after his roommate videotaped him engaged in a homosexual act?" Only two of the fifteen students knew the correct answer, but they all wanted to hear the story.

Tyler Clementi, a gifted eighteen-year-old violinist and freshman at Rutgers University, committed suicide by jumping from the George Washington Bridge after his room-mate socially networked a video of Tyler in flagrante delicto with another boy. Post-quiz discussions were usually fairly lively as I allowed the students to argue that my questions were irrelevant or too hard. On this question, however, there was no such argument. The room was silent.

"I think Facebook and Twitter are evil," I said, hoping to provoke something. They hung their heads, the burden of sorrow heavy upon them.

I'd learned from experience that when something like this happens in class, you have to figure it out on the spot or you'll go home haunted by the confused looks on the students' faces. So I pondered their vibe, I breathed in all their air, and I made a guess.

"How many of you have known someone who committed suicide or tried to commit suicide because they were gay?" I asked. They looked at each other, around the room. All of them knew somebody: a cousin, a friend.

"Utah has the highest suicide rate in the country for males between fifteen and twenty-four," said a girl who I knew had spent some time in therapy.

"Why do you think it happens here more than anywhere else?" I asked.

A returned missionary who hardly ever spoke in class said, "Because according to Apostle Bruce R. McConkie, it's better to be dead than gay."

They all knew the quote, spoken by an apostle, which

meant that it had to be true. But some of the students, about half the class, thought it was horseshit. Even more surprising was that the other half didn't get righteous and shoot them down. Unlike their elders, this generation of Mormons has no fear of or prejudice against gay people, and so when they hear sermons from church authorities condemning homosexuals it sounds to them like something very mean-spirited and crazy. To see this come out in class was like watching a crack open up in the hard egg of Mormon groupthink. It scared them right to their bones because if their leaders were wrong about homosexuality, then maybe they were wrong about other things as well.

For Mormons, like Afghans, the family is the core concept of being, only it's a completely different concept, bordering on science fiction. Mormons believe we are all the spirit offspring of a Heavenly Mother and Father, and that we all lived with them in a "preexistence" in heaven. Then, at a certain point in our heavenly life, we were sent to Earth to experience mortality and be tested in our faith, and also to find someone to marry for life and all eternity.

For life and all eternity a man and a woman are married, following the path toward perfection, eventually becoming gods themselves with their own spirit children somewhere else in the universe, populating another planet very much like Earth, repeating a cosmic cycle. So our god had a father and a mother, and they had fathers and mothers, going back to the beginning of time to the very first Heavenly Mother and Father, whom the Mormons do not talk about. Mormons don't need to think deep into the past because they're busy thinking about the future and becoming a god, keeping the cycle going, and to do this they have to be married to a member of the opposite sex.

As homosexuality has become more accepted around the country, Mormon leaders have become more outspoken in their beliefs that homosexuality is always a decision, a moral choice, and never a consequence of genetics. Why would God make a homosexual? It doesn't make sense to them. Mormon teenagers who realize they're attracted to members of their own sex feel afraid they'll be banished from their families and their church and that God doesn't love them anymore and maybe no one will ever love them. Church authorities play on this fear, telling the children they'd be better off dead.

I turned on the overhead projector and searched the Internet for *The Gathering Storm*, a YouTube video produced by the National Organization for Marriage when our university's president, Matthew Holland, was on its board of directors. NOM is a nonprofit organization that seeks to prevent the legal recognition of marriage and civil unions for same-sex couples. Matthew Holland is the son of another Mormon apostle, just one step below the prophet. The video begins with a scene of billowing thunderclouds and lightning. Five people stand in the foreground. The music is ominous. The actors speak in turn:

There's a storm gathering.
The clouds are dark, and the wind is strong.
And I am afraid.
Some who speak in favor of same-sex marriage have taken the issue far beyond same-sex couples.
They want to bring the issue into my life.

My freedom will be taken away.

I'm a California doctor who must choose between my faith and my job.

I'm part of a New Jersey church group punished by the government because we can't support gay marriage.

I am a Massachusetts parent helplessly watching public schools teach my son that gay marriage is okay.

But some who advocate for same-sex marriage have not been content with same-sex couples living as they wish.

Those advocates want to change the way I live.

I will have no choice.

The storm is coming.

(The music changes to an uplifting horn, and the storm clouds become a beautiful sunrise.)

But we have hope. A rainbow coalition of people of every creed and color are coming together in love to protect marriage.

Some of the students laughed at the video, others were embarrassed, but all saw it as over-the-top propaganda and fearmongering. When it was over they started arguing, and for the first time ever, in all the classes I'd taught, they were arguing with each other and not with me. Some followed the church line and said it's okay to have homosexual desires but it's a sin to act upon them, and that homosexuality can be cured. Others, about half the class, thought that was ridiculous. They spoke up, openly contradicting church authorities. This had never happened before in class and it made them extremely uncomfortable, but they didn't stop. The issue on the line was important, a matter of life and death, and they tore into it, together.

Before they left I said, "This is what's supposed to happen in college, minds coming together and arguing, but it's the first time I've actually seen it happen here. You're brave to speak up, and I want to thank you for being brave because it makes me feel brave as well. I'm tired of being afraid."

After that day almost everybody in the class started working harder on their assignments, and their work got a lot better. I started looking forward to reading their stories and found it easy to write compliments on the pages. This, in turn, made them work even harder. It was like watching a losing team become inspired and start winning, and I was part of the team, the coach, and it felt good.

On two Halloweens in a row Najib was Captain Jack Sparrow from *Pirates of the Caribbean*. He loved Johnny Depp, but even more he loved Captain Jack, and he could look just like him. I don't know why I'm bringing this up now, but it has something to do with why I made him take an independent study where we (Alex, Scott, and I) made him read *The Adventures of Huckleberry Finn* and *The Catcher in the Rye*. I think I was worried he was only learning about popular culture—TV and movies—and had no experience with American literature.

The course syllabus was simple: Read these books and write a paper for each, describing what you learned from reading them. Najib agreed to the deal, but he was worried about it. He'd been neatly avoiding courses that required a lot of reading and writing because reading and writing were his weaknesses and he'd grown up in a place where the weak got killed.

I told him I knew it was a scary thing for him, but that I also knew he could do it.

The first few pages of *Huckleberry Finn* did not give him much confidence. He quickly realized much of it was written in dialect, which he couldn't understand. Najib solved this problem by Tom Sawyering a friend into reading the book out loud to him and then translating. His first reaction when he understood what was going on was, "Why am I being forced to read the story of an uneducated boy who can't even speak good English?"

His interest picked up when Huck fakes his own death and runs away, hiding on Jackson's Island, surviving by his wits. Najib saw that he'd had a similar experience when he went to work selling gum and cigarettes in a war zone. Then, when Huck dresses up like a girl and sneaks back into town to hear what's being said about his death, Najib recognized a kindred spirit, a "professional liar," meaning someone who lied in order to survive through the day, "not worrying about tomorrow."

When Huck teams up with Jim, saying he'll go to hell for aiding a runaway slave, Najib said it was like when he decided to go to work for the United Nations. Everyone on the street in Mazar was telling him the Westerners were bad people who would try to convert him to Christianity or find other ways to embarrass his family, but Najib didn't believe them and he took the job, and his life got a lot better because he made the right decision.

The part in which Jim and Huck start floating down the river, trying to get to the Ohio River and head upstream to freedom—Najib saw this as analogous to his coming to America, suddenly in a wild country, free from the rules of his society. He had to make his own decisions about what was right and wrong, good and bad, based on his own conscience and logic.

At the end of his paper, Najib concluded:

America is no different than Afghanistan. Afghanistan is just behind two hundred years. Afghanistan has a culture in which one race doesn't respect the other, the same culture that America had two hundred years ago. Afghanistan has the culture of wealthy people who buy or own the poor, and America is well known for its slavery. Afghanistan has the culture where the stronger kills the powerless. A warlord decides who should live and who should die. In *The Adventures of Huckleberry Finn*, Mark Twain shows how groups of people carry on certain traditions, like war and murder, for no reason.

Huck talks about his experience of family feud between the Grangerford and Shepherdsons. He asks Buck Grangerford who is only 14 years old "why do you want to kill a Shepherdson?" Buck answers, "it's called feud!" and Huck doesn't even know what feud means. Buck explains and the next question he asks "why there is a feud?" Buck has no idea why his family has a feud with the Shepherdsons, his answer was that this has been going on for hundred years, and there is no need to know the cause. Afghanistan is well known for family feuds and tribal killing, so called "revenge".

In my own family we have had feuds that started hundreds years ago. Most of the today's tribal men in Afghanistan still participate in these feuds, without having any personal reasons, just to carry on traditions. Because of Mark Twain and people like him, leaders like Martin Luther King, Jr. and Malcolm X learned to challenge and criticize a system that is not equal to all races. Even after King and Mr. X were assassinated, others kept going, as result we have an African American president. Afghanistan needs these strong voices of change that never stop fighting. Afghanistan needs its own version of *The Adventures of Huckleberry Finn*.

I'm pretty sure the friend who helped Najib read the book also helped him write his paper because there were too few mistakes in punctuation and grammar, but I didn't call him on it because the thoughts and the voice of the essay were clearly his own, and at least he had thoughts and a voice, which I hadn't seen in most of my regular students.

The Catcher in the Rye was an easier read for Najib, but he didn't like or identify with Holden Caulfield.

I read *The Catcher In The Rye* by J.D. Salinger with a hope that I'd enjoy it and learn something from the characters, but I soon found the main character, Holden Caulfield, annoyed the hell out of me. He is one of those annoying sons of bitches who has achieved nothing, and the entire book is talking about how annoyed he is by everyone around him. If someone has that kind of social phobia, they should stay in their goddamn home, read some goddamn book and bore themselves to death. If he was around today, I don't know if I would call him up and asking him to have a drink with me.

Najib didn't like Holden as a person, but again he started to realize they had a lot in common. In the middle of his essay he compares what happened to Holden in New York City to what happened to him when the United Nations let him go on vacation to Lahore, Pakistan.

It was a big, relatively modern city and Najib was hoping he might get lucky and meet a girl, but instead he ended up walking around for days by himself, getting depressed by the filthy conditions and the meaninglessness of people's lives. Then he describes his encounter with a prostitute.

I woke up at 5 PM and felt energized but disappointed of my discovery of Lahore so far. My room was very hot and I took a shower because I was sweating. I thought I would go outside and maybe find it colder place. On the way out there was a midget setting next to the front desk who said, "Sir, do you need anything? I see you go out and get mangos. Do you like mangos? Let me know if you need anything."

I said, "no thank you I don't need anything, my room is very hot and the AC is not working, I came down to get some cold air."

He said, "this girl likes you," pointing to the girl behind the reception desk who had a rounded face, big eyes and was about nineteen years old.

"thank you, I said. "she is nice"

"no, he said she want to fuck you." I got so nervous I lost all confidence but in the back of my head I was thinking she want to fuck me, she wants to fuck me.

"She said she needs 200 rupees ($2.50), but she'd love to sleep with you," the midget said.

I couldn't wait, I give them midget the money.

"I don't need the money," he said "she will be done at 10pm tonight. she will come to your room and you give her the money."

So I went upstairs with all these thoughts of my father finding out, my tribal people, my job . . . but I wanted the idea of getting rid of my virginity and said it'd be worth it.

The room was so hot, no AC, I opened the window for some wind but there wasn't any. So I took my shirt off and thought I'd take a cold water shower. It was good for a little bit but I was sweating again when I got out. I ate mangos, walked around, took another shower, ate another mango, look outside . . . the time wasn't going fast enough. Finally, she knocked at the door and I almost wet my pants just hearing the knock, how nervous and excited I was. And I was walking to the door, I realized I'd lost the desire. It's as if you are so hungry, but you come to a table full of food, you lose your appetite. So I open the door and see the girl, and she was not what I thought she was. She was twice the size I thought she'd be—I hadn't seen her from behind the desk. I wanted to change my mind. She asked if she could come in, and I was stuck, I couldn't say yes or no, but I really didn't want to do anything.

I said I'm talking with my dad on the phone.

She said, well I'm hungry, so I'll come back.

I've already paid the hotel, so I dropped off my key at the guard at the gate. I checked out and left the hotel. I walked around that town for 12 hours, hearing dogs and smelling shit in the streets, almost feeling homeless and scared because I didn't want to be confronted by some homeless people. And I waited until my bus arrived and it was time for me to leave.

That sounded pretty much like Holden to me. Also, Najib has a little sister, Shoghla, and when they were little they were very close, just like Holden and his little sister Phoebe.

When Najib was eleven, he played hooky from school and came home for lunch. He snuck around the house because he wasn't sure if his parents were there or not.

I went in and walked towards the kitchen to look for some food and saw that Shoghla was cleaning the dishes. She was only five years old back then, a very skinny kid with the most beautiful green eyes. People in our neighborhood would call her a little model and almost every kid wanted to be like her. She was getting ready to start school, but her reading skills were way better than mine and most of my classmates'. She is the smartest kid of her age I had ever seen.

As I was going towards her, I looked back to check the door behind me for my mom or dad and she said, "Don't worry, Lala ('big brother'). No one is home."

I was relieved as soon as she saw me. I immediately said, "I'm really hungry and I need food."

She asked, "Did you not go to school again?"

I tried to avoid the question and repeated myself. "I'm dying and need some food!"

She said, "Do you know if my mom or dad sees you, they will kill you?"

I dismissed her once again and looked through the cupboards and drawers. I thought how she sounded like my mother, so adult by questioning what I was doing.

She went to her room and brought me cake and said, "This is from Lala Rahim's birthday last night." That's all I heard; I instantly attacked the cake and ate as fast as I could while she stood there watching me eat.

When she saw me struggling to swallow, she ran to grab a glass of water. It touched me that she was smart enough at that young age to know I needed help. I wanted to give her a hug but I didn't want to spoil her—or perhaps she was angry with me.

But by the time I was done and was about to leave, I felt her tiny hand hugging me at my leg. She began to cry, saying she loved me and hated it when our father was angry with me. I almost had tears coming into my eyes.

She said she didn't know how terrible school is, but she did know our mother and father wanted us to be educated and go to school. I told her, "No, Khoraki ('little sister'), everyone should be educated. Look at how respected our mother and father are in the neighborhood because they are educated. So it is a very good place. And Lala Rahim loves it there. I am just retarded when it comes to school—I just can't do it very well."

She asked me if I loved our mom, and I said, "Yes, I do." She asked me if I loved our dad, and I said, "Yes, I do." Then she asked, "Can you do something you don't like for Mom and Dad?"

I've never felt so ashamed, embarrassed, and stupid ever before as I was hearing these words come out of the mouth of a little girl.

I thought that was excellent, but the ending of his essay was even better. He writes about the classic passage in the book, the part where Holden talks about wanting to be the catcher in the rye. This is it, from the book:

I keep picturing all these kids playing some game in this big field of rye and all. Thousands of little kids, and nobody's around—nobody big, I mean—except me. And I'm standing on the edge of some crazy cliff. What I have to do, I have to catch everybody if they start to go over the cliff—I mean if they're running and they don't look where they're going I have to come out from somewhere and catch them. That's all I'd do all day.

And this is what Najib wrote:

When I read this I realized that it doesn't matter whether you are rich or poor, American or Afghan, part of growing up is to realize every society has its phoniness in one way or another. The society teaches you what's good and what's bad and they always want you to do the good things when you are a child. When you grow up the same society forces you to do the bad things they wanted you to stay away from when you were a child. For example, when we are young the society tries to keep us away from drugs, killing, and robbing people. When we grow up the same society will sale us drugs, sales us guns and train us how to use a gun and kill people. And like Holden I feel I have seen this reality and I am worried about my own kids or those who are naïve.

There is an MTV show now called *The Jersey Shore* where 6 college girls and boys leave their home for two weeks to go live in a beach house. All they do is work out to get big during the day and at night go to bars to find people to sleep with, and it's the most popular show on TV. Most of my friends watch it every week. In fact they forget about their homework and often get bad grades on their quizzes. It bothers me to see them fail their classes because of a stupid show on TV. If they are not watching *The Jersey Shore*, they are playing video games. It worries me that if this is how they live their lives they might end up working in a gas station or be homeless. I want to tell them to pull their heads out of their asses and study hard to pay back those student loans that they have wasted on video games.

He got it. Najib understood the one part of the book that most young Americans miss. At least I didn't get it when I read it in high school. I gave him an *A* for the course and told him I was proud of him.

"You didn't think you could read or write very well," I said, "but you read these books and understood them and wrote papers that kick the shit out of anything I've seen since I've been here."

"But it was very hard for me," he said. "I worked more to get this grade than in any five of my other classes."

"And unfortunately it doesn't get any easier," I said. "But maybe now you can feel the power of words. You have the power to write, and it feels good, doesn't it?"

"Yes," he said. "It feels good, now that it's over."

I bet this year at Halloween he's still going to be Captain Jack, but that's okay.

This is the fourth graduation ceremony I have sat through, and it may be my last, so I should enjoy it. Matthew Holland, our esteemed president/propagandist, is handing out diplomas, one by one, as the name of each student is called. A tape of the song of the graduation march is playing over and over and over again. Babies are crying; people are yelling and whistling when the name of their son or daughter is called. There's a man with three women sitting two rows down from me. The women all have the same hairdo and makeup, the same style of homemade dress. They are sister wives, polygamists, and for some reason I can't stop looking at them.

Something happened this last semester that I didn't expect and it's kind of scary. I actually enjoyed teaching. There were days driving home on the freeway when I thought, "Whoa, what's happening? Am I losing my edge? Am I going soft?" I think partly what happened is that I became a better teacher, but also the students changed. They're different now than when I started, back in 2007.

Back then when I spoke about the wars in Iraq and Afghanistan, explaining how they were a terrible waste of lives and money and fossil fuels and would only make things worse, there would be one or two students who would get up and walk out of class. They'd hear no criticism of Bush or Cheney or their criminal administration. But the students are not like that now. There's no longer unanimous support for the wars, and they criticize Obama, and not just because he's a black intellectual Democrat. They've become more skeptical of power and authority.

One day, in the spring of 2008, I was talking about how I thought there was a new class of people on the planet, the super-class, who were so rich they could control all major economic and political decisions while suffering none of the consequences except to become even more wealthy and powerful. One student, perhaps the brightest student in class, said, "But we owe the rich so much. They have done so much for us." A few months later, the largest banks and financial institutions in America went belly-up.

Students now come to class more willing to listen to my point of view because they can see they're fucked. They look around and see a shrinking job market, rising prices, growing debt, an energy crisis, a population crisis, a climate crisis, worldwide breakdowns in the rule of law, unwinnable wars against terrorism and drugs—and they know deep in their bones that Facebook, Twitter, and Game Boy will not save them.

Joseph Smith prophesied that in the latter days before Jesus comes back, the U.S. Constitution will be in peril and hang by a thread, and that it will be the Latter-Day Saints who save America from the very verge of destruction. Many Mormons believe this time has come, and their responsibility is to get things ready because Jesus is coming back.

These students have inherited a very large burden, to save the country, and they resent it. Joseph Smith wrote that when the hour cometh they should gird their loins with truth, wear a breastplate of righteousness and shoes made from the gospel, but right now my students just want some hope for finding even a lousy job.

Perhaps I am overinflating what I'd like to see as a new revolutionary spirit. Maybe it's absurd to propose that seeds of rebellion should spring from the most conservative field in the country, but I know for a fact that my students are talking more, arguing more, doubting and questioning more. And if they're doing it here in Orem, Utah, maybe it's happening everywhere. Maybe the university system is a good thing, and in the end the truth will emerge through debate. Leave them alone and they'll figure it out for themselves.

Najib is finally up at the front of the line to pick up his diploma. This is also his fourth graduation ceremony as he's come to every other one just to see what they're like and to dream of being in line, getting to exactly where he is now. He has a Korean friend on the sidelines with a telephoto lens shooting pictures he can send to his family back home. Matthew Holland hands him a diploma and shakes his hand, and I yell and try to whistle as per the local tradition. He made it. He's out of here.

In two months he's getting married to a beautiful Afghan American girl in Fremont, California, and then he might take a job with the U.S. military or the United Nations. He has some offers and a lot of possibilities. He dreams of someday running for president of Afghanistan. It sounds like a fairy tale, but he just might pull it off.

I, however, may be stuck here, in Oremonia. I have four months off before I come back, if I come back, and in the meantime the paychecks keep coming in. If I don't come back, the paychecks will stop coming and I'll have to survive by my wits like Najib on the streets of Mazar or Huck Finn on the river.

The people with me in the stands are paying my salary, but if they knew what I try to teach they would have me fired. I've been trying to get them to fire me, but I've yet to hear one complaint from the administration, and I've never been told what or how to teach. I've been given complete freedom and entrusted with the minds of these young people.

A master stood with his student on the edge of a cliff.

"Jump!" the master said.

"But I'll fall," said the student.

"Jump!" the master said.

So the student jumped.

And he flew.

Scene One

Sunday morning, 1962, a family restaurant.

A husband, wife, and two young sons are eating lunch after attending church. The mother is dressed like Jackie Kennedy—white pillbox hat, long white gloves. The father wears a black suit like Joe Friday on *Dragnet*. The boys have black suits like their father's, and crew cuts, freckles, and glasses that are taped together and hang sideways on their noses. The boys are uncomfortable in their Sunday clothes. The father is uncomfortable with his family.

The mother asks her sons, "Well, what did you learn from the sermon this morning?"

"The minister was saying God listens to our prayers," says the younger son, age five, "so I was praying, asking God to move the light hanging from the ceiling, as a sign. Nothing happened."

"I don't believe in God," says the older son, age six.

The mother is shocked. "Don't say that. There most certainly is a God."

"It's a lie," the boy says. "There is no God." He's angry.

The father is adding up the check, making sure the numbers are correct. The younger son looks out the window to the gas station across the street where a man is filling his tank.

The man bursts into flames.

The son looks at his dad. "They made a mistake," he says, "they overcharged us by $2.38."

The boy looks back to the man in flames, and he's rolling over and over on the asphalt, trying to put himself out.

After the snow falls
all the outdoors
is a refrigerator for my beer.

Notes

For information go to www.prisonerofzion.com.

Most of the stories in this collection were originally published (in slightly different form) as magazine articles. One began as a radio story.

"Over There: Afghanistan, After the Fall" appeared in *Harper's*, April 2002.

"The One Mighty and Strong" began as a radio story for *This American Life*, May 4, 2005. The print version appeared as "The Ongoing Mysteries of the Elizabeth Smart Case" on the *Mother Jones* website, December 14, 2010.

"Where Have All the Taliban Gone? (Looking for the Taliban in Northern Pakistan)" appeared in *GQ*, October 2002.

"Newroz Resolution," originally titled "The War in Iraq," was a report for the *Mother Jones* website in May 2003.

"Straight Up the Face" appeared in *Esquire*, May 1, 1998.

"Human Trafficking in Cambodia" was originally published as "In a Brothel Atop Street 63 (Human Trafficking in Cambodia)" in *Mother Jones*, March–April 2006.

"Rock the Junta (In Burma, a Band of Heavy Metal Christians Speaks of Liberty Between the Lines)," appeared in *Mother Jones*, July–August 2006.

"The Source of the Spell" was published in *High Desert Journal*, no. 12, 2011.

The author would like to thank Larry Massett for his help in editing the manuscript, and United States Artists for a large grant, without which this collection would not have been possible.